The Partnership Way

Riane Eisler

and

David Loye

The Partnership Way

New Tools for Living and Learning

Riane Eisler
and
David Loye

Eisler, Riane Tennenhaus.
    The partnership way : new tools for living and learning, 2nd ed.
/Riane Eisler, David Loye.

    p.   cm.

    ISBN 0-9627232-9-0

    1. Sex role.   2. Social skills.   3. Life skills.   I. Loye, David.
II. Title.
HQ1075.E58   1998
305.3—dc20

THE PARTNERSHIP WAY
Revised Second Edition

Contents

Foreword

Rob Koegel

I'll never forget the day that I first heard about Riane Eisler's *The Chalice and the Blade*. I was visiting an aunt who, when I told her that I was teaching undergraduate sociology courses on gender, asked me what I thought about *The Chalice and the Blade*. When I replied that I had not read it, she said, "How can you teach about gender if you've never read *The Chalice and the Blade?*," and handed me her copy. "This book will definitely interest you," she assured me. "It might even change the way you teach." She was right on both accounts.

Reading about the partnership and dominator models of interaction and social organization in *The Chalice the Blade* and *The Partnership Way* was a moving experience. The term *partnership* spoke to my yearning for mutually enhancing, respectful, and empowering relations. It also evoked my hunger for a caring community that fosters equality, mutuality, democracy, and justice. The term *dominator*, in sharp contrast, triggered an almost visceral aversion to the pain, fear, vulnerability, injustice, and denial that I associate with domination. By clearly naming two distinct social patterns, the partnership and dominator models of interaction helped me to better identify modes of relating that I long for and detest.

These models also enhanced my ability to understand my life and to change it. Sometime in my mid-twenties, I realized that I had internalized certain ways of being and relating that were inconsistent with my commitment to mutuality, justice, and equity. As I became aware of the gap between what I valued and how I acted, I initially felt as though my psyche had been colonized by oppressive social forces. Since then, I've been determined to strengthen habits of thinking, feeling, and relating that enable me to "walk my talk." Like thousands of other people, I have found *The Partnership Way* to be especially helpful in this respect. As Riane Eisler and David Loye put it in their discussion of the partnership and dominator models,

When we use these models to identify what is going on in every area of our lives, we begin to say to ourselves things like, "This is a dominator belief, attitude, behavior, or process — and I want no more of it," or "This is a partnership belief, attitude, behavior, or process — and this is the way I want to be." By developing and using these basic tools — and this basic way of thinking about everything in our lives — we create key building blocks for the partnership future.

The particular form it takes may vary, but there are many people throughout the world who are determined to create "building blocks for the partnership future." Some people focus on the relationships between males and females or parents and children. Others want to infuse partnership into schools, workplaces, health facilities, places of worship, and the media. Still others are yearning for economic, racial, environmental, and international justice.

While the media constantly talks about massive alienation and apathy, millions of people are doing more than dream about partnership. They are involved in organizations that are working to create more mutual relationships, democratic institutions, and equitable societies. Despite their differences, these movements have much in common. They are committed to honoring individuals within an inclusive community. They want personal and social power to be used with and for others, not over or against them. They believe that conflict can be resolved collaboratively and peacefully. Finally, they believe that personal and social change is possible.

If the students I teach are at all representative, many of us believe that there is something wrong with the way we live, but have difficulty understanding the sources of our problems or how to change them. This is where *The Partnership Way* offers invaluable insights. *The Partnership Way* provides a conceptual framework that shows why our problems are not just due to our personal histories, but are rooted in the cultural patterns and social structures that surround us. This book helps us to identify the obstacles to partnership-oriented personal and social action that exist within us, our culture, and our institutions. It also provides an action framework that can support our efforts to work for partnership in our lives and in our society.

It is hard to feel optimistic unless you have a vision that sustains you and provides a life-affirming model of what can be. One of *The Partnership Way*'s most important accomplishments is that it offers such a vision — a vision that can have enormous impact on our lives.

Introduction to the
Revised Second Edition

Riane Eisler

It is with great pleasure that I write this introduction to this new edition of *The Partnership Way*. One reason is that its publication by the Holistic Education Press will ensure that it reaches educators at all levels interested in new ways of learning and living. Another reason is that this new publication offers me an opportunity to update the book, as well as to update readers on new developments on the partnership education movement and my own work.

As the comments on the back cover evidence, over the eight years since its original publication *The Partnership Way* has proven a very useful tool in areas ranging from high schools and universities to community and church groups.

It was to honor the requests for materials by educators and facilitators that *The Partnership Way* was originally written as a practical companion for my book *The Chalice and the Blade: Our History, Our Future*. But *The Partnership Way* also stands on its own as a source of both experiential exercises and discussion questions for use by teachers, parents, students, and anyone interested in personal development and social evolution.

The Partnership Way has been integral to the spread of partnership education through both the Center for Partnership Studies and the International Partnership Network, as well as through countless college and high school classes and community-based groups. One of the pioneers in distance learning, Prescott College, now offers the first university partnership studies program in the United States.

The charts and graphs at the back of *The Partnership Way*, as well as other materials, have been a resource for organizational development consultants and program directors. They have helped organizations in both the for profit and nonprofit sectors more clearly and effectively identify the kind of organizational culture that will support greater creativity and productivity.

I have personally also found *The Partnership Way* extremely useful in my work, both as a consultant to businesses and governments and in the workshops that I am called to give for professionals in fields ranging from education and healthcare to international agencies and socially responsible businesses.

Even more important is that for me writing *The Partnership Way* was one of the first steps in an on-going, ever deepening, exploration of both partnership content (what we learn) and partnership process (how we learn) in primary, secondary, university, and general education.

The Partnership Way offers both partnership content and partnership process. It provides new insights into all aspects of our lives, and tools to help us actualize a better future. Used in conjunction with *The Chalice and the Blade*, it provides new mental maps of our past, present, and the possibilities for our future, culminating in practical action projects. A new development since the first publication of *The Partnership Way* is the release of *The Chalice and the Blade* on audiotape. This can be an exceptionally useful tool, in both formal educational settings as well as community and church discussion groups, when used as an introduction to the exercises contained in *The Partnership Way*.

As I sketch in the section called "The Partnership Way for *Sacred Pleasure*," *The Partnership Way* can also be used in conjunction with my more recent book, *Sacred Pleasure: Sex, Myth, and the Politics of the Body*. This book looks at the hidden history of sexuality and spirituality and charts new paths to power and love. Like *The Chalice and the Blade*, it offers a new worldview or paradigm that takes us beyond conventional polarities such as capitalism versus communism or right versus left to an understanding of two underlying possibilities for structuring all human relations: the partnership and the dominator models.

This new paradigm, summarized in my cultural transformation theory, also informs a second recent book: *Women, Men, and the Global Quality of Life*. I wrote this book in conjunction with my partner and husband, the social psychologist David Loye (also co-author of *The Partnership Way*), and the sociologist Kari Norgaard. Based on data from 89 nations, it verifies one of the central tenets of cultural transformation theory. This is that how a society structures the roles and relations of the two halves of humanity — women and men — is of central importance to everything about it, from its guiding system of values to its family, political, and economic systems. *Women, Men, and the Global Quality of Life* has found practical use not only by individuals but by governmental and nongovernmental organizations because it shows that, as predicted by cultural transformation theory, societies in which the status of women is higher will also tend to have a generally higher quality of life for all. This includes a better distribution of resources, as we see in the Scandinavian nations, where the status of women is higher than anywhere else in the world.

One reason for this higher quality of life is that, as the status of women rises so also do qualities and work stereotypically labeled "feminine," such as caring and caretaking. This seldom noted dynamic is one reason I have during the last eight years focused increasingly on what I call partnership economics. Partnership economics integrates the best elements of both capitalism and socialism but moves further to adequately recognize the value of the caring and caretaking work — including the work of teaching — without which our societies could not go on. In this connection, I have been working with a number of organizations to establish the Clearinghouse for Economic Inventions that Recognize the Value of Caring and Caretaking. The background for this clearinghouse is described in one of the articles available from Holistic Education Press to readers of *The Partnership Way*: the piece called "Changing the Rules of the Game: Work, Values, and the Future."

This leads me to one of the changes in this edition of *The Partnership Way*. I wanted to make more articles available to users of this book. But adding them to the text would have made it unwieldy. So instead we are supplementing the articles found in this edition with additional material that is freely available at the Holistic Education Press website <www.sover.net/~holistic> or by mail from the Holistic Education Press (P.O. Box 328, Brandon, VT 05733-0328) upon request. Other changes are that I have rewritten Session Nine of "The Partnership Study Guide" section and revised the "Partnership Resources" section. I have added to that section a piece by Lethea Erz that provides additional materials on the language of partnership. There are other changes throughout, most of them small, as well as additional readings, including references to two of my forthcoming books dealing with the area that I have primarily focused on over the last four years: the development of curriculum guidelines for partnership education for primary and secondary schools.

These guidelines are outlined in *Tomorrow's Children: Education for the 21st Century*, which also includes many materials that can immediately be incorporated into primary and secondary school classes as well as used for home teaching. A companion work will be *Learning for Living: Fifteen Partnership Literacies and Competencies*. These two books reference materials from *The Partnership Way* that can be of particular use in primary and secondary education.

In addition to my own works — not only books but also scores of articles — publications by many other scholars have used the conceptual framework provided by cultural transformation theory and the partnership and dominator models. One example is "Dominator versus Partnership Cultures: A Potential Framework for

Family Counseling" from *The Family Journal* by Professor Judith Lewis of Governors State University, which quotes from *The Partnership Way*, and proposes the partnership model as a standard for healthy family relations. Another is "The Meaning of Partnership" from *Vision/Action* by Alfonso Montuori and Isabella Conti, which applies the partnership model to management and business.

One of the most interesting examples of work using cultural transformation theory comes from China. A group of scholars at the Chinese Academy of Social Sciences in Beijing applied the template of cultural transformation theory to cultural evolution in Asia and came to the conclusion that the pattern described in *The Chalice and the Blade* for western culture is in critical respects paralleled by what happened in Chinese prehistory. Their book, *The Chalice and the Blade in Chinese Culture*, edited by Professor Min Jiayin, is available from the Center for Partnership Studies, and is described on our website <www.partnershipway.org>.

These have been extremely gratifying developments for all of us in the partnership education movement. Indeed, I have been fortunate during the past eight years in that through my books and invitations to speak, teach, and consult, I have come into contact with countless wonderful women and men dedicated to cultural transformation through their research, writing, and other professional activities. Of particular inspiration to me, as well as help in my educational writings, has been the contact with educators for whom the partnership model has served as a blueprint for a better society.

It is my hope that this republication of *The Partnership Way* will reach many more such women and men. It is also my hope that it will be used by teachers and counselors in teacher and counselor development programs. If we are to stimulate and guide children in their self- development, it follows that we educators need to do the same for ourselves.

I believe that *The Partnership Way*, which offers in depth explorations of our psyches, our society, and our world, is an excellent tool for both personal development and social development. Beyond this, it is a tool for linking like-minded women and men, for bringing together around common interests and concerns a community of partnership educators.

I want to close by saying that I have enjoyed writing, and now again updating *The Partnership Way*, and that it is my hope that you too will find it not only useful but also enjoyable.

— May 1998

WOMEN DANCING. A FRAGMENT FROM 700 B.C. IN GREECE.
LINE DRAWING BY JEFF HELWIG FROM THE ORIGINAL

Welcome to
The Partnership Way!

Welcome to *The Partnership Way*. We hope you will find it a helpful guide to an exciting and enjoyable journey through both the rapids and the shoals of contemporary personal and social change.

The Partnership Way is intended to probe more deeply the choices before us, to help us create more satisfying, more meaningful, less tense, less hurtful, and just plain healthier and more enjoyable options both for our daily lives and our planet.

For a long time many of us have been aware of something basically wrong in our lives, but have found it extremely difficult to do much about it since we could not even name it or clearly visualize another way of being. Indeed, most of what has been taught to us as history seemed to indicate that there is no other way. That has been the underlying assumption, and we all tend to take our basic assumptions for granted, no matter how limiting and destructive they may be.

The Chalice and the Blade: Our History, Our Future by Riane Eisler takes us back to a time before these assumptions became embedded in our psyches and our culture, a time now being reconstructed through a veritable archeological revolution. It shows us that there is an alternative: another way of living, of loving, and of creating a world that is both safe and exciting.

The Partnership Way was created for all those who want to explore these ideas and the information presented in *The Chalice and the Blade* in more depth. In fact, it was created in response to an outpouring of requests from people who have already formed discussion groups to study *The Chalice and the Blade* and its implications for healing ourselves and the world, as well as from university, college, and high school teachers who are using the book in their classes.

We know that to heal ourselves we have to understand what lies behind our symptoms and that this understanding is a prerequisite for any real change. Above all, we have to believe that change is not only desirable, but also possible. And this belief that a healthy alternative exists has to penetrate our unconscious minds, not just on the intellectual but also on the deeper emotional level to enable us to take appropriate action.

This is why *The Partnership Way* is not only a guide to deeper thought and discussion; it also provides opportunities for both imagining and experiencing different ways of thinking and feeling. Even beyond that, it offers suggestions for action, for ways to help accelerate the shift from a dominator to a partnership way of life.

Like *The Chalice and the Blade*, *The Partnership Way* takes us into uncharted territory. It takes us on a new, and at the same time very ancient, path. It is a path of exploration and adventure, a path that is still very much in the making.

We have put together some of the guideposts for this path out of our experience and we have set them forth in the pages that follow. But the actual construction of the path, the specific materials and the labor, will come from your experiences. And it is you who will make the journey your own.

The Partnership Way is your personal guide. You will find in it room to write down your own thoughts and feelings. Because you will probably use it as a guide for groups, it has been designed to facilitate the sharing of your ideas, feelings, and experiences. And since many people worked together in writing this book, we invite you to join us in this participatory process of creation. Please send us your impressions, suggestions, and action-oriented ideas. Strengthening and improving *The Partnership Way* will be a continuing project, a joint challenge and adventure for us all.

— Riane Eisler and David Loye

The Partnership
Perspective

THESE PARTNERS WITH CHALICE ARE FROM A VASE IN THE MUSEUM OF NAPLES
DATING FROM THE MIDDLE OF THE SIXTH CENTURY. THE MALE IS THE GOD
DIONYSUS; THE FEMALE, THE GODDESS SEMELE. THE CHALICE IS DIONYSUS'S
CHARACTERISTIC HIGH-HANDLED WINE CUP, THE KANTHAROS.
THEY ARE SURROUNDED BY THE RIPE WINE GRAPES OF SEMELE.
LINE DRAWING BY JOHN MASON FROM THE ORIGINAL.

How to Use
The Partnership Way

The Partnership Way is a tool for rethinking and restructuring our lives. It is designed to help us clear the ground of old deadwood that impedes our way and put together some of the personal and social building blocks for a more balanced future for ourselves and our children: a world modeled on partnership rather than domination.

The Partnership Way is divided into four main parts: The Partnership Perspective, The Partnership Study Guide, Partnership Resources, and Resources for Course Organizers. Specific guidelines for use are given in each of these parts.

There is still another part, which is yours to create: *The Partnership Way* Personal Journal. We have designed this book with wide margins so you can easily make notes and comments as you read: quotes, cartoons, drawings and pictures, songs, names of books and articles, and so on. In other words, you can create your own partnership resource directory. As you meet with others, you can share these resources to the benefit of all.

The Partnership Perspective

The Partnership Perspective summarizes the differences between the dominator model and the partnership model, and suggests ways to facilitate partnership discussion and study by groups. It has sections on facilitating and communications, as well as on use for colleges, high schools, religious institutions, and recovery groups.

The Partnership Study Guide

The Partnership Study Guide is designed for use by either experienced or first-time facilitators. For those who want to proceed with a minimum of planning and start-up time, the study guide offers a session-by-session plan. Others will want to construct their own plan, drawing from all the materials in this book.

The Partnership Study Guide outlines nine sessions designed for use by community, church, self-help, and other groups. It can also be adapted for college and high school courses.

Those who want to create their own study guide may want to combine selections from the nine sessions with material presented in the second section of the *Study Guide,* called Additional Exercises and Topics for Discussion, as well as from the Partnership Resources.

Partnership Resources

The section called Partnership Resources offers charts and other materials to supplement the nine session series. These resources can also be used by people who want to design their own plan.

As additional resources, articles by Riane Eisler, David Loye, and others on subjects ranging from the family and human rights to economics and technology can be downloaded from the publisher's website <www.sover.net/~holistic>. Readers of *The Partnership Way* who do not have internet access can order the following articles from the Holistic Education Press, P.O. Box 328, Brandon, Vermont 05733.

- Riane Eisler. 1987. Human Rights: Toward an Integrated Theory for Action. *The Human Rights Quarterly* (August).

- Riane Eisler. 1988. Technology at the Turning Point. *Woman of Power* (fall).

- Nafis Sadik. Women, Development, and Population: Highlights from the 1989 State of World Population Report.

- David Loye. 1989. The Partnership Society: Personal Practice. *Futures* (February).

- David Loye. 1991. Moral Sensitivity and the Evolution of Higher Mind. *World Futures* (January/February).

- Riane Eisler. 1991. Women, Men, and Management: Redesigning Our Future. *Futures* (January/February).

- Judith A. Lewis. 1994. Dominator versus Partnership Cultures: A Potential Framework for Family Counseling. *The Family Journal: Counseling and Therapy for Couples and Families.*

- Rob Koegel. 1994. Healing the Wounds of Masculinity: A Crucial Role for Educators. *Holistic Education Review* (spring).

- Riane Eisler. 1995. From Domination to Partnership: The Hidden Subtext for Sustainable Change. *Training and Development Journal* (February).

- Riane Eisler. 1995. A Partnership World. *UNESCO Courier* (September).

- Riane Eisler and Rob Koegel. 1996. The Partnership Model: A Signpost of Hope. *Holistic Education Review* (spring).

- Riane Eisler. 1997. *Foundations for the Future: Four Cornerstones.* Center for Partnership Studies.

- Riane Eisler. 1998. Toward A Partnership Society. *At Work* (January/February).

- Riane Eisler. 1998. *Changing the Rules of the Game: Work, Values, and the Future.* Center for Partnership Studies.

- George Gerbner. 1993. *Women and Minorities in Television: A Study in Casting and Fate.* Report to the Screen Actors Guild and the American Federation of Radio and Television Artists (June).

- George Gerbner. 1988. Telling Stories in the Information Age. In Brent D. Ruben, ed., *Information and Behavior*, Vol. 2. New Brunswick: Transaction Books.

- George Gerbner. 1995. Marketing Global Mayhem. *The Public* 2(2).

We think you will enjoy *The Partnership Way*. It integrates both work and play, both left and right brain, both logic and imagination, both ritual and everyday practicality, both the secular and the spiritual. It has been fun for us to put it together. We hope you will have fun using it.

Resources for Course Organizers

This final part provides background information on *The Chalice and the Blade* that course organizers can use to develop effective promotional materials. It also incorporates current information about the Center for Partnership Studies and the International Partnership Network.

THIS DEPICTION OF A KILLING FROM HORSEBACK, BASED ON A
GRECO-ROMAN VOTIVE RELIEF, SHOWS THE DRAMATIC SHIFT IN THE
CONTENT OF ART THAT COMES WITH THE DOMINATOR SHIFT IN
PREHISTORY. GONE IS THE CELEBRATION OF NATURE, LOVE, AND LIFE.
NOW THE ARTIST, BOTH AS A MASTER OF DEPICTING THE CHANGED
REALITY AND BECAUSE THIS IS WHAT "SELLS," MUST CELEBRATE
DESTRUCTION, HATE, AND DEATH. LINE DRAWING BY JOHN MASON FROM
THE ORIGINAL.

IN CONTRAST TO THE ILLUSTRATION ABOVE, THESE ETRUSCAN FIGURES
SHOW REAL AFFECTION. ETRUSCAN ART, THOUGH NOW ALSO
CELEBRATING DEATH AND DESTRUCTION, STILL SHOWS A STRONG
RELATIONSHIP TO THE EARLIER TIME AND THE ART OF MINOAN CRETE.
THESE PARTNERS WERE IMMORTALIZED IN THE TERRACOTTA OF THEIR
SARCOPHAGUS IN CERVETERI, ITALY, ABOUT 250 B.C.
LINE DRAWING BY JOHN MASON FROM THE ORIGINAL.

From Domination to Partnership

What is a dominator society? And what do we mean by partnership?

Most of us are quite familiar with what *The Chalice and the Blade* identifies as the dominator model. We may not have called it that or seen how its various elements relate to one another, but we have certainly experienced the pain, fear, and tension that come from a way of living based on physical or psychological control.

Such control is part of the dominator model. This model lies at the root of both war and the war of the sexes, both wife beating and child beating, both the exploitation and rape of other humans and of nature.

It is the model that many women and men are today questioning as they reexamine the conventional assumptions about the necessity for war, the ravages of "man's conquest of nature," and the "dysfunctional family" with its stereotypical female and male roles of domination and submission that have caused so much tension, loneliness, and pain.

The partnership model is somewhat harder for us to identify because we have only experienced it in bits and pieces, in fleeting glimpses of what it might be like to live a different way. We have had few guidelines for living in partnership through our schools and universities or our art, books, and other media.

The term *partnership* itself is a good example. Because we need terms to describe a larger system of social interaction based on links founded on mutuality rather than chains of domination and subservience, we have chosen this term, even though until now it has been primarily used to refer to a business agreement or a marriage contract.

On the social level, partnership is the alternative to both patriarchy and matriarchy. On the personal level, all interactions have the possibility of partnership, because interaction based on mutual respect and empowerment, which is the essence of the partnership model, can happen with all kinds of people in all kinds of different settings.

Partnership can be between a woman and a man or between a number of women and/or men. It can be between women and women, men and men, parents and children. It can be between organizations, communities, and nations. It can even be with ourselves, as when we decide that we are going to do everything we can to live in harmony with our bodies and minds. And if we treat nature with respect, recognizing our interconnectedness with our natural habitat, that too is a way of living in partnership.

The basic configurations and key characteristics of the partnership and dominator models are detailed in the charts and graphs on pages 163-175. The readings from *The Chalice and the Blade* assigned in each of the nine sessions outlined in the study guide provide an in-depth view of these two models and how they affect every area of society. And the pages that follow are designed to deepen and solidify this understanding so that we can more effectively identify, strengthen, develop, and disseminate principles and habits of partnership in all aspects of our lives.

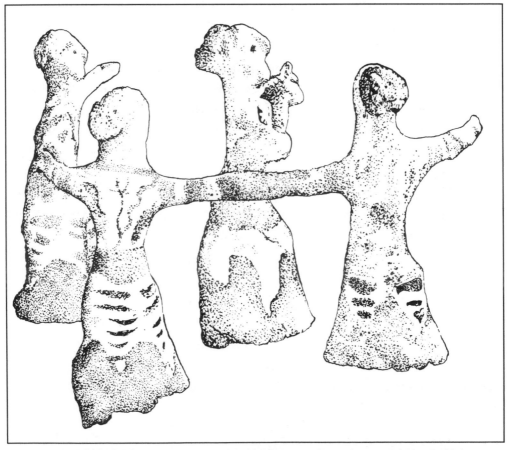

POTTERY FIGURES OF WOMEN DANCING TO THE MUSIC OF A LYRE, FROM PALAIKASTRO, ABOUT 1400 B.C. LINE DRAWING BY JOHN MASON FROM THE ORIGINAL.

The Partnership Way
for Group Facilitators
and Teachers

Facilitator is a new word for leader. It describes a way of leading appropriate for a partnership rather than a dominator world.

The conventional definition of a leader — the one we have been taught in our schools, where we learn about famous generals, emperors, and kings — is that a leader is a man who gives orders, who controls others. Today, as we are trying to shift from a dominator to a partnership society, this old "strong-man" model of leadership is being challenged.

In both the political and corporate worlds we are hearing more and more about a new kind of leader or manager. This is someone — a woman or a man — who inspires rather than commands, who brings forth the best in others rather than cowing them into submission; someone who elicits creativity and trust rather than rote obedience and fear. Clearly, this is a style of leadership suitable for a partnership rather than a dominator society.

The partnership way for leaders is still largely uncharted territory. We simply have not been taught how to lead in partnership. Quite the contrary, in popular parlance we still speak of 'leaders" and "followers." But not so long ago, people thought (and acted) in terms of "rulers" and "subjects" We have already come a long way.

Today there is a growing literature on new styles of collaborative leadership. There is also a growing tendency to see a group leader as a facilitator who makes it easier and more fun for people to work in groups.

1. We gratefully acknowledge that some of our guidelines are adapted and excerpted from the excellent Guidelines for Leaders in *Cakes for the Queen of Heaven*, and we thank both its author, Shirley Ranck, as well as its publisher, the Unitarian Universalist Association, for permission to use them.

The guidelines that follow are primarily designed for those who do not have facilitator experience. But we think they will help all facilitators to more easily and enjoyably organize and facilitate partnership study groups.

Forming and Nurturing a Partnership Group

To form a partnership group, a good way to start is to talk about *The Chalice and the Blade* with friends and neighbors, at school, work, church, or wherever you meet. You may want to ask people if they would like to meet in what is essentially a wellness rather than a therapy group: an exploration of more productive and satisfying thought, feeling, and action.

An effective study group can vary in size from two to as many as thirty or even forty people. But if you have a large group, dividing it into smaller units, as outlined in the material that follows, is very important.

There is no guaranteed process by which a facilitator and a group create an environment that is supportive, open, and growth-producing. There are processes, however, that have been used effectively by group facilitators in a variety of settings, and we share those processes here. Experienced facilitators will be familiar with those listed and may add others. We share these guidelines out of our collective experience in the hope that they will be helpful to you.

Choosing the Facilitators

Because working in partnership is the central theme of *The Partnership Way*, we strongly recommend choosing two cofacilitators. And because partnership between the female and male halves of humanity is the foundation for a partnership society, we suggest that the cofacilitators for groups that include both women and men be a woman and a man.

These two cofacilitators may be the original organizers. Or they may be chosen at the first meeting. Or the group may want to choose different facilitators for different sessions. In that event, it is essential for continuity and smooth functioning that two people take responsibility for overall administration.

Creating the Partnership Environment

Working in partnership, the cofacilitators are responsible for finding a location and creating an environment conducive to partnership interaction. You may have to alternate locations, but for continuity it is better to find a place that can be used throughout the sessions.

Try to arrange for a comfortable, attractive meeting space appropriate to the size of the group. The physical setting can contribute greatly to harmonious interaction among participants. If change in the meeting place becomes necessary, be sure to let the group know well in advance.

Try to work in a circle and use a space large enough to make this possible. This way everyone can see everyone else and partnership is more easily facilitated.

Supplies and Other Resources

You will need a number of basic supplies for each meeting. These include at least two large newsprint pads and a number of large-point felt-tip pens (black and also some colors, for more effective presentations). The best way to use the newsprint pad is with an easel, as this ensures easy visibility for the whole group. You should also have some masking tape in case you want to put up sheets of newsprint for people to see their input. These supplies are easily obtained at art supply stores.

Other materials, such as visuals (books, artwork, photos, and slides) will help add richness to the meetings. Audio materials such as tapes may also be useful. (Tapes of Riane Eisler and others talking about related subjects are available through the Center for Partnership Studies.)

Where appropriate, the use of music at the beginning and the end of each session can do much to create a relaxed and open atmosphere. Not only the cofacilitators but also members of the group can take responsibility for selecting and bringing tapes and CDs, as well as visual materials.

Responsibilities of the Cofacilitators

While every member of the group is an active partner, the cofacilitators have the primary responsibility for making this an enjoyable sharing and learning experience supportive of personal growth and positive social transformation.

To ensure this, it is important that you:

- Plan to be at all sessions. Continuity of leadership is important in building group cohesiveness. If you are cofacilitating and must be absent, let the group know in advance. Whenever a group facilitator is absent, interrelationships must be rebuilt.

- Plan to arrive before the other group members and have all equipment and materials ready for the session. This helps participants to feel comfortable and contributes to an organized, relaxed flow in the group process.

- Try to begin and end the sessions on time. Ask group members to let you know if they expect to be late or miss a session. Absences raise questions and concerns about the well-being of the missing person. A group does nor function effectively if there are questions about a member's absence.

- Read through the outlines of the nine sessions before the series begins. Review each session's outline before the session begins. Being familiar with what is to be covered in the current and subsequent sessions will enable you to sense when you can go into a topic in more depth and when you will need to move on.

- Be prepared to write summary statements at the end of each session.

- Bring your copy of *The Chalice and the Blade* and ask the participants to bring their own copies to all meetings, as this makes it possible for people to find passages that have been of particular importance to them and share them with the group.

- Keep notes of what happens each time in the group: the kinds of experiences related, the insights learned, what seemed to excite the participants most. Use this information to help you plan later sessions and to remind the group from time to time of the journey they have been taking.

It is essential that notes of each session be kept and that a provision be made for this in advance. This is an important supplement to the use of the newsprint pad to write down key words and ideas. These notes make it possible for participants to review the ground they have covered, and serve as the basis for suggestions for improvements and additions to future editions of *The Partnership Way*.

Working in partnership, the cofacilitators are also responsible for:

- checking that the meeting place is available and readied for each meeting

- getting names, addresses, and phone numbers of all participants

- making announcements and sending notices if necessary

- encouraging participation

- facilitating summaries and closures at the end of each session

- passing out participants' names, addresses, and phone numbers to group members.

We would also appreciate cofacilitators sending names and addresses of participants and any suggestions for *The Partnership Way* to the Center for Partnership Studies.

Encouraging Participant Involvement

The Partnership Study Guide provides session plans for a nine-week series. These plans suggest many possibilities and will have to be adapted to the needs and wishes of the members of the group. It is a good idea to encourage group members to participate in planning from the beginning. Specifically, they can be encouraged to:

- lead their own opening and closing ceremonies

- create some of the activities

- contribute additional readings and other materials.

To the extent that each participant can take an active role in creating the study group, the experience of working in partnership will be greatly enhanced. During the sessions, participants can do the following:

- be responsible for opening, closing, and/or facilitating parts of sessions

- report on supplemental readings

- take notes

- bring poems, music, books, tapes, and other resources.

The variations are endless. The primary intent is to offer practice in *shared leadership*. Enjoy and be creative, open to the richness and surprises that shared leadership can offer.

Facilitating Experiential Learning

Since real learning is not just intellectual, the study guide also suggests experiential exercises for each session, often in the form of guided visualizations. For participants to benefit from these exercises, the cofacilitators should give special attention to the following elements.

Relaxation

Participants should be helped to relax and open themselves to new ideas and experiences. One way to do this is to ask people to close their eyes and take three deep breaths (inhaling and exhaling slowly), and then for thirty seconds to a minute to simply observe their breathing along with any thoughts and feelings that come up. It is very important that the cofacilitators be centered and that they speak very slowly, as this in itself has a relaxing effect. In this and other ways, they themselves model and communicate an open and relaxed state, creating a relaxed and safe environment for the group.

Preparation

It is a good idea to write out notes for the guided visualization beforehand. In fact, for all but the most experienced facilitators, it may be best to script everything, including the opening and closing directions.

Opening

For example, to begin each guided visualization, the facilitator tells the participants that she or he (or another member of the group) will take them on a guided visualization. Ask them to find a comfortable position to sit in, paying attention to how their bodies feel; to close their eyes, take a deep breath, and relax their bodies. Then ask them to just observe their thoughts as they go by, allowing their minds to relax too, gradually emptying their minds. Tell them to keep breathing slowly and deeply and that they should take a few moments to do this. Then begin the guided visualization, once again making sure to speak very slowly.

Closing

At the end of the guided visualization, allow for a few moments for people to stay in touch with their feelings and the thoughts and images evoked by the experience. Then ask them in a soft voice to open their eyes, and perhaps to stretch, before sharing what they experienced.

Questions

Posing specific questions about participants' experiences during the exercise can help them formulate their thoughts to share with the group. The study guide suggests some questions to use.

Time for Sharing

The most important part of guided visualizations and other experiential exercises is the opportunity to share the feelings, thoughts, and images the experience has evoked. Each person needs adequate time — depending on the exercise, at least five minutes per person. *Therefore, in groups larger than six to seven people, it is essential that the group divide itself into smaller subgroups for this experiential work in order to make enough time for everyone.*

Dyads are the most effective subgroups for sharing. This is almost the only way to go for large groups, since the next step after the small group sharing is for the larger groups to reconvene so that at least some of the members can summarize their experiences for the larger group — and this clearly takes longer in larger groups. Where group size and time parameters make it possible, it is best if all participants can share their experiences with the larger group. A nice — and usually quicker —

variation on this is to have each person's dyad partner summarize for the larger group what the other member shared with her or him.

It is essential that the cofacilitators communicate to the group that during experiential work, group members must truly listen to each other. This is not just a question of common courtesy; it is the basis for establishing a sense of belonging founded on mutual trust. To develop trust, group members must feel that everyone will be heard and will be reasonably safe from criticism. Trust is basically feeling that one is not being controlled, that even if someone does not like another person's opinion, he or she is willing to hear it.

Particularly in dyads doing experiential sharing, it is essential for the listener not to interrupt the speaker. This is something the cofacilitators should stress every time. And they should also encourage all the participants to work on their listening skills. (See section on Partnership Communications below.)

Keeping it Going

Each group will have its own needs and preferences. Here are a few suggestions that facilitate group partnership process.

- Use the session plans flexibly; they are guides to adapt to the needs and preferences of the group. Encourage group members to express their suggestions for different formats or content. Try to maintain an even balance between activities and didactic input. It is usually a good rule of thumb to engage group members in exploring their present knowledge and feelings about an issue or topic before presenting new information.

- If your group is larger than six or seven, you may want to divide up into groups of two, three, or four for the discussion after the experiential work, with each group having a chance to report back to the whole on what they have discovered. This will ensure that everyone has a chance to be heard. At each session, members can work with a different group in order to experience the richness of the wisdom of all the participants, if everyone agrees to this.

- Try to know each member of your group, and help the group members get to know each other. Taking time to build group rapport and trust is an essential component of every session. It can be helpful at the beginning of each session to invite participants to tell of an experience of the past week that gave them new insight into how the partnership and dominator models affect our lives or to relate a personal observation they wish to share with the group.

- Respect each person's contribution or right to keep silent and remind the group to do likewise. Guarantee the right to pass. It is important for group rapport and trust that members not feel pressured into sharing more than they are ready to reveal.

- Strive to keep a single individual or small group from dominating the discussion. If this occurs, ask yourself what is happening. Has the topic released an issue of great concern? Are there individuals who feel threatened and are using this as a means to keep control? Uncovering a hidden agenda can be a key to new understanding.

- Help the group to keep focused. If individuals start to talk about other things, remind them of the subject or task, and make a note of their concern so that it can be addressed later or privately. Encourage group members to help you keep the focus. This can be a group responsibility.

- Be sure that insights and learnings arrived at by the group are gathered up and given expression, and that personal sharings are honored in some way. Provide a time in each session when this can be done or use the opening and closing ceremonies, where appropriate, to accomplish this purpose.

- Support group trust by having participants agree to keep personal confidences that have been shared within the group. No one wants her or his story retold elsewhere.

- Be sensitive to the potential emotional impact of this material on participants. Strong emotions may surface. Anger and rage may spring from unknown sources and mask pain. Tears and expressions of anger are clues to underlying strong emotions that people may have difficulty acknowledging and articulating. Give yourself and the other person time and room to express emotions. Make a decision about how to act when participants become emotional. Do not confuse support with agreement. You may support a person in her or his grief, fear, or anger, and be critical about what she or he does with it. Strong emotions are energy and as such can be channeled into constructive action. Ask questions, use your intuition, challenge assumptions, and make suggestions.

- Seek a balance in your own participation. This balance is dynamic. Encouraging others' participation is usually more fruitful than inadvertently being the one everyone turns to as the expert.

- Take your time. Allow participants time to reflect at each session on their thoughts and experiences since the last meeting. Listen to the group and encourage clarification. Try to hear the questions behind the ones posed. Pay attention to new agenda items and interests.

Pacing the Sessions

The sessions will be more effective if the cofacilitators attend to and guide their pace.

Breaks

We all know that no matter how interesting a lecture or discussion may be, if it goes on too long, we tend to tune out. Since each session is designed to last several hours, adequate breaks are essential. Plan a ten- to fifteen-minute break at approximately the middle of each session. Be sure to schedule it at a natural breaking point, such as between the experiential work and the discussion.

Special Events

We all like to have something special to look forward to. So you may want to plan with the group to have a special event during the series — a potluck meal or informal party. This type of event works well close to the midpoint of the series. Plans need to be made, and if possible everyone should contribute something. It is important that someone coordinate this, and that a number of group members take responsibility for bringing all necessary equipment and food and/or making sure everyone who promised to bring something is clear on it and plans to follow through. It may also be nice to have some music for this session or some other way of making it special.

Those groups that cannot have a special meeting might want to make one of the sessions longer to provide time for some special refreshments, either after the meeting or during a longer midpoint break. This special event and the more informal party atmosphere are a good way to strengthen individual friendships as well as the feelings of belonging to a group, and to simply have some fun.

Closings

Instead of (or in addition to) a midpoint special event, group members might want to plan a meeting or party at or after the last session. If this is not possible, members may want to create a special closing ceremony for the final session. A special event or closing provides a sense of closure and accomplishment, and an opportunity to celebrate your shared experience and learnings and to say goodbye — or, even better, to make plans to continue meeting, either informally or as a group.

Partnership
Communications

Though we have stressed communications in the preceding section, these skills are so generally essential outside as well as within discussion groups that we want to further focus on them here. In other words, we're thinking here of what helps build partnership in families, on the job, in schools, and everywhere else two or more of us are gathered.

Because the usual way of looking at communication is as a one-way street, as an act of imparting information to others, most of what we read about communication skills focuses on the communicator. But clearly it takes more than one to communicate. There is not only the writer but the reader, the receiver as well as the sender, the listener as well as the speaker.

In face-to-face personal communication, the role of the listener is critical. If we look at personal communication as a partnership where two or more people take turns talking and listening, we see that to build good relationships the listener's part is just as important as the speaker's. And if we recognize that good relationships are based on mutual trust, we also see that good listening skills are an essential ingredient.

Therefore, the communication guidelines that follow emphasize listening skills.

Active Listening

It is very important that people in a group truly listen to each other. For example, when working in dyads, a cardinal rule is that the speaker not be interrupted.

But listening is more than just not interrupting. It is acknowledging through one's active attention that the other person is being heard.

Perhaps most important is that people who are sharing their feelings be assured that they will not be criticized for having such feelings.

A very good way to ensure that you are truly listening to others — and that they know you are really listening — is to play back to them, in your own words, what you have just heard them say. You can say, for instance: "Let me see if I understand your point. You are saying that _____. Do I understand that correctly?"

While you put the other's views in your own words, it is important that you do not include any words or phrases that *evaluate* or *comment on* what the other person said. It should be a simple playback to be sure you heard and understood the point that was being made, whether or not you agree with it. The other person then has the opportunity to correct your impression if it was not quite accurate or complete. Once the understanding is achieved, the conversation can move on to comments, responses, or statements of other or additional views.

Respectful Communications

When people are expressing opinions, it is of course important that others feel free to disagree and to say so. But there is such a thing as agreeing to disagree. And the key is not to make others feel that they are being controlled. In other words, people need to understand that even if others do not like their opinion, they are willing to hear it. That's what communication is about.

That is not to say that free communication means absolute freedom of speech. In both law and custom, there are essential limits, such as the prohibition against falsely yelling "Fire!" in a crowded theater or inciting violence against members of different racial or religious groups.

Free communication means respectful communication. And respectful communication is essential in partnership study groups, particularly during experiential work. Active listening needs to be encouraged and nurtured not only by the cofacilitators but by all members of the group as well.

The Partnership Way for Colleges and High Schools

Many college professors and high school teachers have adopted *The Chalice and the Blade* as an assigned or supplementary text for courses ranging from history, sociology, and women's studies to peace studies, futurism, and philosophy. Therefore, we have also designed *The Partnership Way* for use in these more formal settings.

The suggestions offered in this book can easily be integrated into a course plan prepared by the teacher, or they can be used as the basis for a section of the curriculum or for a whole course.

The Partnership Way is specifically designed to facilitate the integration of materials dealing with the history, analysis, problems, and aspirations of *both* women and men into the general curriculum. It is also useful as a basis for courses that focus on the social foundations of peace, particularly classes on Western civilization, women's studies, and peace studies. It provides materials to meet a variety of curriculum needs.

Teachers using *The Partnership Way* in a college course will find that the Discussion Topics sections in the study guide offer a rich selection of questions for study and discussion. Teachers in high schools and some college courses will probably also want to use the experiential exercises. The Partnership Resources section provides charts on the partnership and dominator models that students in classes ranging from English literature and current events to sociology, psychology, and women's studies will find useful.

For the teacher interested in helping students learn to live and work in partnership, *The Partnership Way* is an important resource not only because of its substantive content, but also because it integrates partnership ideas with partnership process.

As teachers ourselves, we feel that one of the most important things we must teach children and young people is how to work in partnership. We have found a great hunger for such learning among students. For example, when one of us taught a course at UCLA on the social and legal status of women, the students were asked to choose partners to work together on term projects for which they would be jointly responsible. Some of the students were doubtful at first. But at the end of the course they almost unanimously endorsed this method. It was less tense, they said, than the usual one-against-one competitive mode. In fact, it was not only more enjoyable, but more effective. *They could not understand why this was the only class they had ever taken that had actually helped them to work together in teams!*

Clearly, the lack of this kind of education for teamwork (except in highly competitive situations such as sports and debates) has caused many personal and social problems. It is also increasingly recognized as a source of major difficulties for the business and corporate sector, where teamwork is being found to yield far greater productivity and job satisfaction than the old mode of individual competition.

The tools offered in this book will aid teachers and others who want to help their students live and work in partnership and provide the basis for a very important kind of research. This is what we call partnership research — a participatory action-oriented approach designed to identify, strengthen, and create partnership models for all aspects of our lives through group data gathering and testing.

We also invite you to use Riane Eisler's book *Tomorrow's Children: Education for the 21st Century*. This work, specifically geared to educators, provides comprehensive guidelines for developing partnership curricula and lesson plans for primary and secondary schools. It offers an integrated approach for curriculum design that gives students the opportunity to use the partnership and dominator models as analytical lenses in classes ranging from the natural and social sciences to history, art, literature, and current events. It is gender-balanced and multicultural/pluralistic, with a strong environmental emphasis that highlights our interconnection with nature.

In a time when so many young people feel alienated and hopeless, *Tomorrow's Children* offers a scientifically grounded and hopeful perspective on what it means to be human, as well as knowledge and skills to help actualize both our human and social potentials. This work will be of particular use to high school teachers, but will also be useful for university courses, not only in teacher and counselor education but also in many other departments. *Tomorrow's Children* crossreferences to materials in *The Partnership Way*.

We especially invite you and your students to contribute to this exciting new approach to research, teaching, and learning.

The Partnership Way for Religious Study or Independent Spiritual Development

While most major religions have at their core a partnership spirituality, they also have a dominator overlay. As a result, the essential message of our interconnectedness, powerfully expressed in the Jewish and Christian traditions by prophets like Joshua and by Jesus, has all too often been distorted in the way religion has been taught and practiced.

One of our most urgent tasks today is to strengthen the partnership core of religion. This book is designed to help us do this. It provides materials for individuals seeking a strong spiritual dimension in their lives as well as for religious study groups in the Catholic, Protestant, Jewish, Moslem, Hindu, and Buddhist traditions and congregations of the Church of Religious Science, Unitarian Universalists, Bahai'i, and others who combine teachings from all these traditions.

It is evident that we cannot build a true morality based on the subjugation of one half of humanity by the other. Partnership is an important tool for integrating and translating into action the "softer," more "feminine" teachings of most great religious and spiritual figures; it shows us how to do unto others as we would have them do unto us. Above all, it is a tool for the reintegration of spirituality into our lives, not as something we can only access through dogma from "higher up" but, as Jesus and many mystical teachers have taught, through *gnosis* or direct knowledge of the divinity in all aspects of life.

The partnership approach makes it possible for us to reclaim an important but still largely suppressed part of our religious history. For example, it allows both women and men to explore the Catholic veneration of the Virgin Mary as a continuation of ancient traditions where the deity was imaged as a Great Mother who had *both* divine daughters and sons. In Jewish tradition, it explains the presence of the female Shekina at the center of Hebrew mysticism. It also illuminates the centrality of "feminine" values such as caring, nonviolence, and compassion to the teachings of Jesus.

Most important, it offers us an integrated approach to our spiritual heritage. By providing a better understanding of our earliest forms of worship, it reconnects us with millennia-long traditions when the chalice — the power of love and illumination — was the governing image. And whether we are Jews or Christians, Hindus or Moslems, pagans, agnostics, or atheists, it helps us reclaim for ourselves and our children a more life-celebrating and life-enhancing kind of spirituality, firmly rooting it in a more just, harmonious, and ecologically balanced kind of society.

Because it is built on partnership between the female and male halves of humanity, a partnership spirituality supports the contemporary movement to reinstate women in religious leadership roles. At the same time, it reinstates the feminine in religious imagery and theology, greatly enriching both women's and men's spiritual lives. Indeed, by clarifying the partnership character of so-called "primitive Christianity," it brings many of the core ideas and practices of early Christianity back to life. And by providing us with new/old myths and images that recognize and honor the great spiritual potential of both women and men, it offers us a spirituality that gives new meaning and purpose to our lives.

The Partnership Way is designed for use by all religious denominations, theological seminaries, and other groups and individuals that share the concern for helping us to move from a dominator to a partnership society. It is our hope that it can help us lay the spiritual foundations for a world where *hochma* and *sofia* (the ancient feminine appellations for wisdom) can truly rule and *agape* (or sisterly *and* brotherly love) can guide our interpersonal and international relations.

The Partnership Way for Addiction and Recovery Groups

All over the United States, and now also in other parts of the world, women and men are coming together to help themselves and their loved ones recover from patterns of addiction and codependency. Only a short time ago addiction was associated with only alcohol or drugs. But today we are beginning to recognize, in the words of Anne Wilson Schaef, that ours is an addictive society: that patterns of addiction — be it to compulsive eating or to work, to mechanical sex or to abusive relationships — are more the norm than the exception. Along with this has also come the growing recognition that addiction and its correlate, codependency, stem from what psychologists call dysfunctional families: families in which children arc routinely physically and/or emotionally abused.

How did all this come about? Why would so many people (seemingly the vast majority) get themselves into these miserable situations? It does not seem to make much sense, considering that avoiding pain and seeking pleasure are the most basic human (as well as animal) impulses. And why would they stay in such a painful fix?

Armies of psychiatrists, psychologists, and social workers have been trying to answer these questions by looking at people's personal and family histories. That is certainly an important first step.

But when millions of people are enmeshed in dysfunctional addictions and codependent relations, the problem is clearly not just personal, but social. We have to look not just at our personal and family histories, but at our social and cultural history. The basic question that we have to address is, what in a social system can make people literally go against their natural pain-avoidance and pleasure-seeking impulses?

The Partnership and Dominator Alternatives

The dysfunctional family — based on control and fear — is the kind of family that is required to maintain and perpetuate what we have called a dominator society:

a way of organizing social relations held together by control through fear, denial, and ultimately force. Sometimes referred to as the traditional or patriarchal family, it rank orders human relations through dominator/dominated roles, beginning with the stereotypical dominator/dominated roles women and men are required to play. This was the kind of family that went along with traditions such as slavery, serfdom, and the "divine right of kings to rule."

It was in this dominator family that both boys and girls were conditioned to fit into a dominator society, learning to repress and deny their pain and anger, to deflect it against "inferior" or "dangerous" people, and to carry feelings of mistrust and betrayal into all social relations, thus keeping the whole system in place. And both mothers and fathers then passed these patterns of family relations on from generation to generation, thus unwittingly maintaining not only the dominator system, but also the pain and misery we are now beginning to recognize as stemming from dysfunctional homes.

The exciting thing is that today so many people are no longer accepting ways of thinking and living that not so long ago were viewed as "just the way things are." It is exciting not only for the immediate personal lives of those involved, but for society as a whole. For by challenging ways of relating based on denial and control, we are effectively challenging the very foundations of a dominator society. And by questioning old adages such as "spare the rod and spoil the child" and the inevitability of the "war of the sexes," we are beginning to leave behind the habits of behavior required to maintain a social system where "strong-man rule" (be it in the home or state) and the subordination of women (and all that is considered "feminine" or "weak" in men) is considered normal and necessary by both women and men.

The Partnership Way is designed to help take this process an important step further. It is designed to help women and men working in Twelve-Step and other recovery groups more effectively deconstruct not only the belief systems, but also the day-to-day practices, that have imprisoned us in unhealthy and painful ways of relating to ourselves and others. Most important, it is designed to help us move from deconstruction to reconstruction, to the creation for ourselves and our children of more satisfying and humane partnership alternatives.

Just as the dominator family is the training ground for living in a warlike, male-dominant, and basically authoritarian (or dominator) society, the partnership family is where we can learn to live in a more peaceful, just, and mutually satisfying way. Here neither women nor men have to be imprisoned in the rigid straightjackets of roles that deny them part of their humanity. Here the bringing up of children is not mainly through fear or negative conditioning but primarily through the positive conditioning that rewards helpful and responsible behaviors. And here both little girls and little boys have the opportunity to develop self-esteem, along with attitudes and behaviors that make it possible for them to live with others in the mutually respectful and cooperative way required for a pluralistic and truly democratic, or partnership, world.

Self-Help Programs

The basic premise of self-help programs, such as Twelve-Step programs, is that through partnership — through sharing of feelings and ideas, mutual respect, and, above all, mutual empowerment — we can heal ourselves. But the construction of a partnership society requires more than recovery, it requires renewal and growth.

The materials that follow offer a rich source of both new information and experiential work that can enrich and broaden Twelve-Step and other self-help programs. In addition, the nine sessions can be utilized to form parallel partnership groups. And for those who are ready to move beyond personal healing to the essential social healing, they offer tools for both personal and social transformation.

It is our hope that in helping us understand that our problems stem not from our personal shortcomings or perversities, or even from those of our mothers and fathers, but rather are rooted in an unhealthy and imbalanced dominator social system, *The Partnership Way* can help us more successfully deal with our negative feelings, particularly our feelings of guilt and shame. It is also our hope that *The Partnership Way* will be a catalyst for developing positive feelings, images, and actions that can more effectively guide our recovery, both emotionally and spiritually.

We recognize the enormous contribution of the Twelve-Step programs and believe it is essential that we learn to acknowledge and seek guidance from our higher selves, whether we call this God, Goddess, or higher spirituality. At the same time, we are also concerned about an element of disempowerment in the constant reiteration that we are powerless. It is certainly true that as addicts or codependents we are powerless to control our situations as long as society keeps driving us to addiction and codependency. But it is also true that working together we have the power to change ourselves and society — and that unless we do, we will indeed remain powerless.

For power in the best sense is not control and domination over others, but the power to create for ourselves and our loved ones better partnership ways of relating. *The Partnership Way* is designed to help us reclaim that power.

AN ANCIENT CONVERSATION. BASED ON A VOTIVE RELIEF
DEDICATED TO XENOCRATEIA, FIFTH CENTURY B.C.
LINE DRAWING BY JOHN MASON FROM THE ORIGINAL.

THE EARLY LOVE OF MUSIC CAN BE SEEN IN THIS SKETCH (LEFT) BASED ON A
CYCLADIC FLUTIST SCULPTED IN HIGHLY POLISHED WHITE MARBLE FOUND IN
KEROS, NEAR AMORGOS. THIS ONE DATES BACK TO THE 3RD CENTURY B.C. A
HARPIST CARVED IN WHITE MARBLE (RIGHT), ALSO FOUND IN KEROS,
ALSO DATES TO THE 3RD CENTURY B.C.
LINE DRAWINGS BY JEFF HELWIG FROM THE ORIGINALS.

The Partnership
Study Guide

IN THESE POTTERY DANCERS OF 1400-1100 B.C., WE SEE THE ORIGIN OF THE
MODERN CRETAN DANCE "PENTOSALIS." MADE FAMOUS BY THE MOVIE ZORBA THE
GREEK, DANCERS CHARACTERISTICALLY HOLD EACH OTHER'S SHOULDERS. IN EARLY
TIMES THIS "PARTNERSHIP" DANCE WAS PART OF RELIGIOUS CEREMONIES.
LINE DRAWING BY JIM BEEMAN FROM THE ORIGINAL.

Introduction to the Study Guide

This introduction is intended to help set the stage for the sessions that follow. Facilitators may want to integrate some of this material into their opening remarks at the first session.

Ours is a time of crisis, but also of opportunity. It is a time of great personal and social upheaval, a confusing and difficult time because we are realizing that many of the conventional ways of doing things are not good for us. But precisely because we are taking a fresh look at so many of the old givens — such as war, racism, sexism, wife battering, child beating, and rape — it is also a time of new hope and opportunity.

Many of us are reexamining ways of thinking and living that not so long ago were seen as "just the way things are." In the process, we are also beginning to see that we can create for ourselves more satisfying ways of living, that we can shift from a dominator to a partnership society.

In his book *Global Mind Change*, Willis Harman (1988) states: "Throughout history, the really fundamental changes in societies have come about not from dictates of governments and the results of battles but through vast numbers of people changing their minds — sometimes only a little bit." He points out that economic, political, and even military institutions persist because they have legitimacy, and that legitimacy comes from the perceptions of people. People give legitimacy and they can take it away. A challenge to legitimacy is probably the most powerful force for change to be found in history.

What we are now learning about the real possibility of constructing a partnership society powerfully challenges the assumptions that have given legitimacy to the dominator model. Even beyond that, by joining together to use this knowledge, we not only change our inner images of reality but we also begin to change every aspect of our world.

Goals of the Study Guide

The goal of this study guide is to help us see the barriers to positive personal and social change, both inside and outside of us, that until now have been so taken for granted they have been invisible. By moving us beyond the probing of our personal and family histories to a new understanding of our social and cultural history, these sessions can help us see that our story as human beings is not as limiting and negative as we have been told. By exploring millennia-long traditions belonging to a time when the mainstream of our cultural evolution oriented primarily to a partnership rather than a dominator model, these sessions can also help us see that the chronic tensions, miseries, and bloodbaths of the last five thousand years have *not* been due to human nature but rather to a dominator detour.

A second goal of this study guide is to help us recognize patterns — that is, relationships between mutually reinforcing parts of a system. In the case of the dominator patterns, this helps us cut through the conventional confusion that has obscured our root problems. In the case of the partnership system, it helps us lay the foundations for new structures, new habits, that can better our lives and our world. Above all, it can help us see that how we relate to ourselves and to others on the personal level and the kind of society we live in — and even whether our global system can survive at this critical evolutionary crossroads — are inextricably interrelated.

A third goal is to help us build on these foundations, to construct for ourselves a new framework for positive personal and social action. Specifically, then, the most important purpose of this study guide is to help us *do* things differently. The purpose is not only to help us see that a more satisfying way of living and loving is possible, but also to experience that by working together in partnership we can integrate principles and habits of partnership into the deepest recesses of our hearts and minds. This can then provide the necessary foundations for a functioning partnership society.

Process

But how do we learn to live, work, and love in partnership when so much of what we have been taught — from ideas like "a man should be the boss in his home" to stories and pictures idealizing "heroic conquest" — are thought and action scripts for domination rather than partnership?

The first step is to reexamine what has been presented to us as "traditional" stories and images, and at the same time learn about very different traditions that lasted for many thousands of years. This gives us a new contextual framework, offering us alternatives to what we have been taught is "just the way things are."

The second step is to use this new contextual framework to create *new stories and images* with which to write for ourselves *new thought and action scripts*. For it is through these new stories and images that we can give voice and shape to a powerful new vision of our present and future that can help us learn new habits of thinking, feeling, and acting.

We all can think of an example of change in our personal lives, whether it involved quitting smoking, or forming a new habit like eating less fat or sugar or regularly doing some kind of exercise. Even the most entrenched social attitudes can — and do — change, like the once-prevalent idea that slavery is only natural. Moreover, our most powerful social institutions can be altered, like the shift not so long ago from "divinely ordained" despotic monarchies to democratic republics.

But to make these changes, it is not enough that we analyze and discuss what we want to change. Learning involves not only reason but also emotion and action. To learn new and better ways of living, loving, and working, we have to involve *both* our linear, logical learning abilities and our emotions and intuitive faculties. Particularly, we need to improve our ability to see interconnections or patterns in a system as a whole if we are to take appropriate action for change. This is why these sessions are designed to integrate both intellectual and experiential learning as the basis for developing new modes of action.

The outline for each session includes a summary of its goals and a list of discussion topics. Equally important are the suggestions for getting started and closing, which are usually more experiential. These help to put us in direct touch with ourselves on a deeper level of our feeling and life experiences. By combining, on the one hand, focused study and stimulating discussion and, on the other, the imaging and experiencing of new patterns of thought, feeling, and action, we can more quickly learn to integrate ways of living, loving, and working in partnership into our day-to-day lives.

Structure of the Study Guide

The Partnership Study Guide is designed to serve a wide variety of users. For individual users or for facilitators with little experience, it can be used with a minimum of preparation. Or it can be a rich resource for more experienced facilitators who want to design their own study and discussion plan.

The *Nine-Session series* offers nine structured meetings. Each session consists of ten parts: Goals, Readings, Materials, Preparation for Facilitators, Getting Started, Further Exercises, Discussion Topics, Supplementary Readings, Preparation for the Next Session, and Closing.

Session 1 provides a process for the members of the group to get acquainted and together formulate commonly agreed-on goals and procedures. We recognize that in certain settings, such as university classes, it may be difficult or impossible to integrate this session into curriculum design, but we highly recommend its inclusion as it sets the tone for a partnership learning process.

Each session offers at least one experiential or participatory learning exercise and a number of discussion topics to choose from. Facilitators can easily plan a series by simply selecting the appropriate experiential exercise and/or discussion topics in each session. You will have to decide how much time you have and choose accordingly. You may want to use some of these suggestions in the order given; you may want to alter the order; or you may want to substitute some of your own goals, readings, exercises, and discussion topics.

The section Additional Exercises and Topics for Discussion provides materials for those who want to design their own longer or shorter series and/or supplement the basic materials in the nine sessions.

While the Partnership Study Guide offers a variety of options, it is basically geared to three levels of exploration:

- Individual growth and relationships

- Implications for our society and its institutions

- Our relationship to the natural world or cosmos

Not all the levels are addressed in every session, but the facilitators should keep them in mind during discussions and encourage the group to consider each level wherever appropriate.

It seems to be the nature of the partnership process that once you are under way with the right people, a natural flow tends to take over. Those who choose to be part of such a group are true explorers. Enjoy each other and the joint adventure that lies ahead!

Session 1
Getting Acquainted

Goals

1. To get acquainted with one another.

2. To examine our goals for the series.

3. To begin to visualize better personal and social alternatives.

Readings

None for this session.

Materials

Large newsprint pads, easel, felt-tip pens, masking tape, name tags for group members, a sign-up sheet with room for group members to write names, addresses, and phone numbers.

Optional: A candle, a sturdy and safe candleholder, refreshments.

Preparation for Facilitators

*   Prepare some introductory remarks or adapt the Introduction to the study guide for this purpose. Be prepared to introduce yourselves and to discuss the study plan with the group. Make a list of overall goals on newsprint, using the goals in the Introduction as guidelines and incorporating your own ideas.

*   Familiarize yourselves with the outline of the nine-session program so you can tell the group briefly what it covers. (It is a good idea to write the session titles on newsprint.)

- Familiarize yourselves with the material under "Facilitating Experiential Learning" in the earlier chapter entitled "The Partnership Way for Group Facilitators and Teachers."

- Whenever possible, set up seating in a circle, as a circle helps to unify the group and makes conversation flow more readily.

Getting Started

It is important to make sure members of the group get acquainted in a way that connects with the reason they have come and with their expectations.

A good way of doing this is for the facilitators to begin by introducing themselves, telling the participants why they brought this group together, and introducing the series. They can use their own introductory remarks or an adaption of (or excerpts from) the Introduction to the study guide. It is recommended that this segment take a maximum of ten to fifteen minutes.

The members of the group are then asked to briefly introduce themselves and tell the others why they are here and what they would like to take back with them. As the group members are sharing, it is important for the facilitators to record key words and phrases on large newsprint sheets. The phrases that are recorded will be used in the process of forming group goals and are also needed for the facilitators to write a summary of the first meeting.

Setting Group Goals

When members are sharing their goals, they should be encouraged to frame them in positive terms — in other words, in terms of what they want rather than what they don't want. After everyone else has expressed their hopes and expectations, the facilitators can then share what they expect to get out of the sessions. This too is recorded on the newsprint. *It is very important for the facilitators to have thought this through and to be able to clearly communicate a positive image of the expected outcome again, very specifically, what you want rather than what you don't want.*

This would also be an appropriate time for the facilitators to put up the goals for the series they have prepared before the session and to invite the participants to compare and notice the similarities and differences between the overall goals the facilitators have just put up and the individual goals that the participants have shared.

Then the participants are asked to decide which goals this particular group feels are most important in relation to their stated hopes and expectations. Again, it is important for things to be stated in positive terms and as specifically as possible. This is the first step in a participatory or partnership process and can be used as an example during future sessions.

Facilitators may want to remind members that the goals may change as the sessions go on. Also, this is an appropriate time to increase the participants' awareness of how the partnership process worked for them.

Suggest that they do not evaluate the process in terms of "good" or "bad" but simply take an observer position. Sometimes it helps to explain that taking this position is like watching a movie and just observing the action. Then the participants can take their observations away as food for thought and perhaps become aware of what in themselves or others either facilitates or impedes the partnership process.

A good way of closing this section could be for facilitators to take a few minutes to play the opening of *The Chalice and the Blade* audio tape for the group. This will do two things: first, the lead-in, read by Marc Allen of New World Library (the producers of the audio tape), tells some of what has happened since the original publication of *The Chalice and the Blade*. Second, the voice of Riane Eisler reading a portion of the Introduction to *The Chalice and the Blade* sets the stage on a personal note for what follows.

In those situations where it is appropriate and time permits, the group may want to take a short break now. Obviously, each group will be different and the amount of time it has taken to get to this point in the session will vary depending on the size of the group and the skills of the facilitators.

Further Exercises

Those groups that have enough time left can try any or all of the suggested exercises that follow. You, as facilitators, will have to decide how to delete, combine, or integrate these suggestions.

If the group has taken a break, when it reconvenes the facilitators may want to suggest that this part of the meeting, as well as future sessions, open with a brief ceremony.

Ideas for Ceremonies

The idea of a ceremony or ritual may seem strange to some people at first. But in many ways we all use rituals in our daily lives: the handshake as a greeting ceremony; the exchange of cards; blowing out candles at birthday parties to celebrate our birth; or the clinking of glasses to toast the pleasure of being together.

Developing a ceremony to open meetings can serve as both a way of helping to form group bonds and taking the participants into a more relaxed and centered space.

However, this ceremony should not be imposed and should be handled with sensitivity.

One of the facilitators could light a candle and explain that this is probably a very ancient opening ceremony, since the light and warmth of fire has linked members of a community since the dawn of human society. Or you might ask the group if they want to do a brief breathing exercise. One of the facilitators would then ask people to close their eyes, take three deep breaths, and observe their own breathing for a few minutes.

There are many possible variations, but the aim is to help people feel they are embarking on a special adventure together and to relax. We all are very busy and lead complex lives. It is important to help the members of the group leave behind their tensions and cares, at least for a while. After the brief ceremony or breathing exercise, the following process is a good way to help people get in touch with each other and with their feelings.

Visualizing a Partnership World

When the participants are relaxed, ask them to close their eyes and visualize, as clearly as possible, what the world would be like if women and men were equal partners. Invite the group to be as specific as possible. What would they see, what would they hear, what would they feel? If they were writing, producing, and directing a movie of a world where men and women were equal partners, what would that movie be like?

The following questions may be of help:

- What do you think our lives would be like if there were equal partnership between women and men?

- How would it affect our self-image as women and men?

- How would it affect our family relations?

- Would international relations differ? Race relations?

- Would our religious institutions change?

- How would it affect our education?

- Would the corporate sector and the workplace be altered?

- How would it affect social priorities?

- Would there be changes in entertainment, art, and humor?

- What kinds of things would be considered funny?

- What would be most highly valued and rewarded?

When you can sense that people are finished, ask them to open their eyes and divide into dyads and take ten to fifteen minutes to share their "movies" with each other.

Sharing Visions

Each person takes a turn being the "storyteller" while the other is the listener. Some people will take to working in dyads easily, but for some it will be unfamiliar and they may start off by feeling uncomfortable. It may therefore be a good idea for the facilitators to deal with this openly, to invite group members to view it as a new adventure, something like traveling in a foreign country with different customs. It may feel alien at first, but therein lies the fun and richness of new discovery.

You may also want to suggest that individuals pair up with someone they don't know. Emphasize that the job of the listener is to listen and not to evaluate or judge the "story" of the other person.

This experience will help to establish that first important one-to-one link: the kind of closeness that is most easily felt with just one other person. It gives everyone a chance to be heard as well as to listen. Perhaps most important, it builds trust and a feeling of belonging. Individuals can begin to understand others' realities with their similarities and differences.

To stay on schedule and make sure there is enough time for the larger group discussion, the facilitators should set a time limit (perhaps ten to fifteen minutes) for the dyad work and also remind the dyads when it is time to begin to wind up. When the participants return to the larger group, the sharing continues.

This discussion will naturally lead to the question of what the major obstacles to equal partnership between women and men are. A good way to focus the discussion and also end on a positive note is to talk about areas where these obstacles are beginning to be addressed, such as family therapy and the current reexamination of dominator/dominated sexual stereotypes and the idealization of "man's conquest of nature." Also ask participants to think of areas that are not yet being addressed and focus on one such area.

Discussion Topics

Since this first session is geared toward establishing group connections and introducing the participants to partnership group process, there may not be time for discussion questions. If there is time, you could introduce one of the discussion topics from Session 2 or choose one from the Additional Exercises and Topics for Discussion section.

Supplementary Readings

None for this session.

Preparation for the Next Session

Remind participants of the readings for the next session and ask them to bring their own copies of *The Chalice and the Blade* to each session. Ideally, participants should also have and bring their own copy of *The Partnership Way* for the additional readings and for their own Partnership Way Personal Journal. Otherwise, facilitators need to be responsible for a great deal of copying for handouts, beginning with the readings assigned for Session 2.

Facilitators should also plan to bring an example of a chalice and a blade to the next meeting and could suggest to participants that they can also do so if they want. (This can be anything from a kitchen cup and table knife to a collapsible camper's cup and hunting knife.)

Closing

In preparation for closing the meeting, you may want to ask the group if they want to close with a ceremony. Explain that people may need to relax after this intensive journey. Sharing a closing ceremony and formally opening the circle can help make the transition back to everyday life easier.

You may want to use blowing out the candle as a signal that the session has concluded. Some groups may want to repeat the breathing exercise or play a tape of relaxing music. Whatever feels comfortable to the participants is the way to go.

When and if the participants decide on a ceremony, set the stage for the next session and take care of any unfinished business before using the ceremony to close the session.

Helping Our Mailing List Grow

Please be sure to send a list of the names and addresses of participants to the Center for Partnership Studies, Box 51936, Pacific Grove, CA 93950, right after the first meeting so they can be added to our mailing list. If new members join the group, please update the list.

Session 2
Crisis and Opportunity

Goals

1. To begin to look at the kinds of relationships we experience every day and how the current crisis in gender roles is also an opportunity to rewrite our personal and social life scripts.

2. To begin to identify elements of partnership and dominator models in our own experiences.

3. To begin to explore how our personal and global problems relate to a dominator system and how a lot of our contemporary crises are also opportunities for accelerating the movement to partnership.

4. To explore the meaning of the chalice and the blade as symbols and their implications for our world and our lives today.

Readings

The Chalice and the Blade: Introduction

The Partnership Way: All dominator and partnership model charts and explanatory materials in the Partnership Resources section in this guide ("The Partnership and Dominator Models: Basic Configurations," "The Partnership and Dominator Models: How to recognize them" ... and "Everyday Partnership Action Chart").

Materials

Newsprint pads, felt-tip pens, masking tape, name tags for group members, an example of a chalice and a blade.

Optional: A candle and candleholder, refreshments.

Preparation for Facilitators

- Remember to bring your copies of *The Chalice and the Blade* and *The Partnership Way*. Put up the summary statements of the last meeting for people to refer to as they discuss their thinking and experiences since then.

- Write the title of this session on newsprint and be prepared to write summary statements of this session as well.

- Optional: If group members have agreed, make copies of the sign-up sheet passed around at the first session, to hand out to group members so they have one another's phone numbers and addresses.

Getting Started

An alternative to opening with a ceremony would be for people to take turns reading a particularly meaningful passage from the readings for the session. An addition or alternative would be to play some short passages from the audio of *The Chalice and the Blade* read by Riane Eisler.

After the agreed-on opening, a good way to get right into the material for this meeting is to use the following free-association exercise.

Free Association with *The Chalice and the Blade*

Ask the participants to free-associate by saying whatever comes into their minds as they focus on first the chalice and then the blade that you or group members have brought, with one of the facilitators listing the associations on a sheet of newsprint. Someone is sure to mention nurturing and feeding in response to the chalice. Someone else may talk about it as a spiritual symbol of actualization and transformation. Its association with the "feminine" and with the ancient Goddess as a source of life and nurturance may also come up.

The blade will probably be seen by some as a symbol of taking rather than giving life. Others may talk of it as expressive of a culture like that of some of the Indo-European barbarians that overran Europe (who, as UCLA archeologist Marija Gimbutas writes, literally worshiped the lethal power of the blade). Still others may relate the blade to the still-prevailing "conquest of nature" mentality, and in turn link that to our equation of "masculinity" with conquest — be it of women, other men, or nature.

Some of the discussion will undoubtedly focus on how the blade has become the symbol of a dominator view of power in a society where blades are mythologically associated with the "masculine." From this perspective the chalice represents a more "feminine" view of power: power from within oneself; power with, rather than over, others; enabling and supportive rather than dominating and destructive power.

But there will probably also be some discussion of an aspect of the blade that transcends and antedates the dominator system. This is the blade as an early tool for harvesting wild grains and tanning hides — a tool used by and associated with women *and* men. This can easily lead to the question of sexual stereotypes of "masculine" domination and action versus "feminine" subservience and passivity, and how these stereotypes are today being challenged.

Everyone can join in this discussion even if they have not given these things much thought before, and this way the meanings come directly from the group. Also, each person can be asked to free-associate the meanings of these symbols to specific experiences and patterns in her or his own life.

Further Exercises

Either as a supplement or as an alternative to exploration of the chalice and blade symbology opening exercise, participants can be asked to close their eyes and wait for images to come that they associate with first the chalice and then the blade.

They can be asked to pick up a chalice or imagine picking one up and holding it. Ask them, "How does it feel?" "What can you do with it?" Then they can do the same with the blade. The group can talk about these images and perhaps draw them on the newsprint. They can be asked to note the differences in the feelings and images they associate with each item.

The participants can then be asked to put these images in the context of the alternatives of the partnership and dominator models and how our definitions of what is "masculine" and "feminine" would be different in each of these models. They could also be asked to think of how, in a partnership society, masculinity would not have to be equated with conquest and domination and how in such a society qualities such as caring and compassion as well as assertiveness and self-expression could be considered appropriate and desirable for both men and women.

Participants could also be asked to think of all the images of weapons that are portrayed on television, and the frequency with which they are seen. Facilitators can make a list on newsprint. Then ask the group to come up with all the images of the chalice they can think of and the frequency with which they are portrayed. Make a list on a separate piece of newsprint. Give people a few minutes to notice the differences and then ask them to imagine what it would be like if the chalice imagery of enfolding and nurturing were seen more frequently and the blade images of cutting and destruction were reduced.

Discussion Topics

Select one of the following three topics for discussion to begin with. Use another if time permits.

1. Many of us are exploring new ways of relating to one another. We are discovering that the old models of relationship do not really work, and are seeking better alternatives. A way of cutting through some of the confusion is to look at our exploration as an attempt to shift from dominator/dominated to partnership relations (see charts on pp. 193-208 in the section Partnership Resources) and to ask ourselves to look at our own relationships from this new perspective.

The following questions can help stimulate this discussion:

- When have you been dominated? What did it feel like?
- How did you cooperate with this?
- What do you think you might do differently now?
- When have you been a dominator? What was that like for you?
- What were its advantages? Its disadvantages?
- When have you participated in a partnership? What was that like for you?
- What were its advantages? Its disadvantages?
- How do you think you received social support for a partnership relationship?
- How do you think it was opposed or undermined?

2. The Introduction to *The Chalice and the Blade* shows that we have been taught a limited vision of alternatives. For example, we tend to think that the opposite of patriarchy is matriarchy without realizing that they are both dominator models and that the real alternative is partnership.

We have also been taught to divide the world into opposing camps such as religious vs. secular, capitalist vs. communist, developing world vs. developed world, light-skinned vs. darker-skinned races, and so on. To gain real insight into how these systems and structures affect humanity, it is useful to look at the dominator or partnership aspects in each of them.

The following questions can help stimulate this discussion:

- How does the distinction between patriarchy and matriarchy differ from that between the dominator and partnership models?

- How does thinking in terms of partnership and domination cut through conventional polarities such as religious vs. secular or communism vs. capitalism?

- Name or identify partnership and/or dominator aspects of particular religions, philosophies, and political structures, focusing particularly on contemporary trends toward partnership and the dominator resistance.

Allow plenty of time to discuss these questions, not only in this session, but also in later ones, because our awareness deepens and broadens over time.

3. Many of our contemporary global crises — such as environmental pollution and the threat of nuclear holocaust — are the result of the emphasis a dominator system places on so-called masculine values of conquest and domination. For example, in the United States almost 60 percent of every tax dollar has gone to financing foreign intervention, nuclear weapons, and other military expenditures, with only a fraction of it left (after interest payments on the national debt) for human services. And in the poorest, most overpopulated, and most warlike and violently repressive "developing" regions of the globe such as parts of the Middle East and Latin America, women and so-called feminine values such as caring and nonviolence are most suppressed and despised.

The following questions address this topic as well as the growing awareness that a fundamental shift in priorities is essential.

- Why do you think that all over the world today there is so little social priority given to so-called women's issues?

- Do you think we would have massive overpopulation if women had free access to both birth control technologies and equal educational and job opportunities?

- Do you think the fathers who today see their role as including the traditional "feminine" mothering will be less likely to consider warfare "manly" and "fun"?

- Why do you think the modern feminist movement has met with so much resistance from both the extreme right and left?

4. Many of our contemporary crises are also opportunities to develop new and better ways of living, working, and loving. For example, on the personal level, the changing roles of women (and men) are sometimes confusing. But they are also opening many new options to both women and men.

On the social level, we have seen the piecemeal replacement of old dominator forms (like the despotic rule of kings over their "subjects" and of men over the women and children in the "castles" of their homes) with more democratic families and states, where linking rather than ranking is the primary organizational principle. But such fundamental social changes cannot happen without a certain degree of social and personal dislocation.

- Why do you think some people focus on the "breakdown" of the family and others recognize that if new partnership family forms are to emerge, the older dominator family forms cannot remain in place?

- Why do you think that people are more likely to deny and suppress their real feelings in a dominator society?

- How do you think the modern development of psychology relates to the movement toward a partnership society?

- How do you think current psychological priorities support or impede the movement toward partnership?

- How do you think the civil rights movements and the struggle against racism and colonialism are central to the modern partnership thrust?

- How do you think rapid technological changes have worked in creating for us both crises and opportunities?

Where the group is large and has broken into smaller groups, it is especially important to have a general discussion of what emerged in the small groups and to tie it back to the Introduction to *The Chalice and the Blade,* especially the concept of the two models of society — dominator or partnership — based on ranking or linking.

Also be sure to write on the newsprint the major themes that emerge in this and subsequent sessions. This will provide a kind of group history, and these sheets can be put up at the beginning of each meeting to provide the group with a sense of continuity and identity.

Ask the members what was particularly helpful and interesting in this session and what they would like to repeat or do differently next time.

Supplementary Readings

None for this session.

Preparation for the Next Session

Remind participants of the readings for the next session and ask them to bring materials to share, such as books with good illustrations of Paleolithic and Neolithic art (see Supplementary Readings at end of Session 3), pictures and/or reproductions of Goddess figures, evocative music, or a tape of a relevant talk or discussion. Alexander Marshack's *The Roots of Civilization* would be a good source for pictures of "wrongway weapons." (See also line drawing on page 55 below.)

Closing

As established during Session 1, or select from earlier suggestions.

AN EARLY IMAGE OF THE GODDESS FOUND CARVED ON A ROCK AT LAUSSEL, FRANCE, FROM PALEOLITHIC TIMES. THIS ONE IS UNUSUAL IN THAT SHE IS HOLDING WHAT APPEARS TO BE A HORN OF PLENTY IN THE SHAPE OF A CRESCENT MOON — A SYMBOL LATER ASSOCIATED WITH ARTEMIS OR DIANA, HUNTRESS AND LADY OF THE BEASTS.
LINE DRAWING BY JEFF HELWIG FROM THE ORIGINAL.

Session 3
Our Hidden Heritage

Goals

1. To develop an awareness of the modern reappraisal of Neolithic agricultural societies and evidence that strongly suggests that in these societies the world was imaged as a Great Mother who had both divine sons and divine daughters, relations between women and men as well as between men and men, and women and women were generally equalitarian, and war was virtually unknown.

2. To reexamine our personal and cultural values and assumptions in the light of this ancient alternative model.

3. To reexamine our feelings about the female and male bodies in light of this information.

4. To continue the reappraisal of our feelings about masculinity, femininity, and power in terms of the information presented in the readings for this session.

Readings

The Chalice and the Blade:
      Chapter 1, "Journey into a Lost World: The Beginnings of Civilization"
      Chapter 2, "Messages from the Past: The World of the Goddess"
      Maps and charts, pp. 163-175.

Materials

Regular supplies plus art books and pictures, particularly of Goddess images, and other materials brought by group members (see Session 2's section on preparation for this session).

Preparation for Facilitators

Same as for Session 2.

Getting Started

Refer to last session's summary statements for some continuity and an opportunity for fresh insights. When appropriate, bring the group to this session's focus: our hidden heritage and its implications for our present and future.

The Paleolithic "Venuses" and the countless Neolithic Goddess figurines, statues, and other images are astonishing to most people. This is why it is important to have such pictures at this session. Begin by passing them around. Looking at these images where the sexual parts of a woman's body are often depicted as sacred is an effective way of accessing different ideas and feelings about our bodies and the consequences for our values and social organization.

After the participants have had a chance to look at these pictures, ask them to reflect on how we have been taught to view women's and men's bodies. In mixed groups, a good way to approach this question of our feelings about the female and male body is to ask the women and the men to form separate groups. This makes it easier for women and men to talk openly of their feelings and begin to reexamine how they have been taught to think of women's and men's bodies, as well as to get in touch with their feelings about their own and others' bodies. It may also be effective to split the smaller groups into dyads.

Free Association on Women's and Men's Bodies

In dyads, two women can share with each other what it felt like growing up and becoming aware of their changing bodies.

- What did it mean to them to "become women"?

- Was their first period presented to them as a "curse" or as welcome and natural?

- What were the body images presented to them as ideals?

- Were they taught to think of their bodies as a source of pleasure to themselves or to others — namely men?

Working in dyads may also make it easier for men to look more deeply into their feelings about women's bodies.

- Were they taught to see them as objects to be taken and used?

- How did the way they learned to look at their own bodies and their own sexuality relate to this?

This sharing of feelings about women's bodies and thus also images of women and femininity will inevitably bring out strong feelings. For some women, there will be painful feelings — feelings of inadequacy, of somehow failing to "measure up."

Discussion of these experiences usually goes easily into all the ways advertising tells us we are not OK but need to be thinner, smell better, have a different hair color, etc., and all the things various religious groups teach girls about covering or being ashamed of their bodies.

Men dealing with similar questions will also have strong feelings. For instance, the dominator model's rejection of the life-giving powers of the female body may translate into a rejection and alienation of all our bodies. This was the case in Western society, where the Church condemned all that is carnal, especially female bodies but also to some extent male bodies — all flesh.

It is also helpful for both men and women to examine how our images and feelings concerning the male body sharply differ from those about the female body. Thinking about the male body may yield an image of strength, action, and instrumentality, and a great deal less concern as to whether and how a particular male body differs from an arbitrary cultural ideal of what is "beautiful."

It may also be of interest to note how we generally pay great attention to and place great importance on the advantages of the male body, such as height and stronger bones and muscles, while the advantages of the female body, such as developed breasts, better-protected genitalia, the uterus with its creative capacity, and the lesser vulnerability to disease and to inherited weaknesses and disorders, tend to be overlooked or considered less important.

At some predetermined time, the women and men come together again into the larger group and share their feelings and thoughts. This discussion should easily lead into the whole issue of the "superiority" of men and the system of values that goes along with this.

Further Exercises

Values and Gender

The following questions may be helpful in exploring the issue of values and gender.

- Why should so-called masculine values such as conquest, exploitation, or domination (be it of women, other men, or nature) have social priority?

- What lies behind the contempt expressed in much of our literary and folk tradition for women and so-called feminine values such as nonviolence and compassion?

- What really is a sissy (weak sister) or "effeminate" man?

- Is expressing empathy and caring really a weakness?

- How do you think the devaluing of women as a group with different physical attributes relates to the devaluing of other races as groups with different physical attributes?

In a society where the highest value is assigned to the power to give and sustain life incarnated in women's bodies,

- Would women suffer from "penis envy"?

- Would sex be "dirty"?

- Would killing people and destroying property in warfare be idealized?

- Would men be ashamed to be caring or "soft"?

Rites of Passage

A good way to end this portion of the session is to ask the participants to take a few minutes to imagine rites of passage for girls and boys that would assist their emergence into womanhood and manhood in a partnership society.

These questions may be helpful:

- What would these partnership rites of passage be like for boys and girls?

- In what ways could they be designed to celebrate and honor the unique differences of each gender?

- How would they differ from rites of seclusion during menstruation and after childbirth as a protection from "pollution" in tribes where women are dominated by men?

- How would you feel as a woman if you went through a rite of passage that was empowering and spiritually uplifting?

- How would you feel as a man going through such a rite?

- Try to imagine this for yourself and for your daughters and sons.

- How would you begin to design such rites and then work for their use and acceptance?

As in every session, the facilitators should use the newsprint pad to record the feelings and ideas shared by the members of the group.

Discussion Topics

1. How does the way we have been taught to think of our bodies as women and men affect

- Our self-image?

- Our ideas about sex?

- About religion?

- About race relations?

- About power?

- About other major aspects of our lives?

- Why do you think the pregnant female body, once so central, is so rare in dominator religious, artistic, and media images?

2. In Goddess-centered societies, what was likely to have been woman's self-image? Man's self-image?

- How do you think these societies would react to some of our current images of "sex goddesses"?

- What are your reactions to the Paleolithic and Neolithic female images?

- Do you think the artists were women or men or both?

3. What view of humanness is reflected in the many androgynous images of the Goddess from the period of prehistory?

- What are the implications of a reverence for the lifegiving and sustaining powers of both the male and the female?

- How might an androgynous view of divinity (ultimate reality seen as Mother and Father) affect the way we view ourselves? One another? The "feminine"? The "masculine"? Social and economic values and organizational structures?

4. How might relations between women and men have differed in societies that regarded a Divine Mother as the source of all life and the progenitor of both divine daughters (Kore, Persephone) and divine sons (Horus, Attis)?

5. Discuss the persistent belief that civilization began with the warlike, hierarchic, and patriarchal empires of the Sumerians, the Assyrians, and the Egyptians, and that earlier social orders were "precivilizational" or even "savage."

- What are the essential characteristics of civilization?

- Were the agricultural societies of the Neolithic period civilized in the modern sense? Why or why not?

- How do prevailing models of the necessary attributes of civilization reflect and reinforce the dominator system?

- What are the implications of the modern rediscovery of an ancient alternative?

This discussion may lead to the notion of "the selfish gene" and other biological and social theories on the "inevitability" of male dominance and war in the civilized order. Reading aloud excerpts from *The Nature of Human Aggression* or *Not in Our Genes* may prove useful (see the Supplementary Readings list that follows). These themes will continue to be important in later sessions.

6. How do shared cultural images of our deep past affect our view of the nature of human beings and human society? Of our present and future? Of masculinity and femininity?

- Consider the familiar cartoon pictures of club-wielding cavemen dragging women about by the hair. What role do these and other such misconceptions of our ancient heritage play in maintaining the dominator order?

Supplementary Readings

For full titles and citations, see the References at the end of this book. This list is for those who want more to read on any aspect of this session.

Fritjof Capra, *The Turning Point*

    Riane Eisler, *Sacred Pleasure* (particularly chapters 1 and 3)

    Marilyn Ferguson, *The Aquarian Conspiracy*

    Marija Gimbutas, *The Civilization of the Goddess*

    Marija Gimbutas, *The Goddesses and Gods of Old Europe* and *The Language of the Goddess*

    Min Jiayin, *The Chalice and the Blade in Chinese Culture*

    Mara Lynn Keller, "The Eleusinian Mysteries of Demeter and Persephone: Fertility, Sexuality, and Rebirth"

    R. C. Lewontin, Steven Rose, and Leon J. Kamin, *Not in Our Genes*

David Loye and Riane Eisler, "Chaos and Transformation"

Alexander Marshack, *The Roots of Civilization*

James Mellaart, *Catal Huyuk*

Ashley Montagu, *The Nature of Human Aggression*

Vicki Noble, *Motherpeace*

Merlin Stone, *When God Was a Woman*

Ethel Tobach and Betty Rosof, eds., *Genes and Gender*

Preparation for the Next Session

Ask the group to bring pictures of the architecture, frescoes, sculpture, and jewelry of Minoan Crete. Also, the cofacilitators and others may want to bring pictures of some of the nineteenth- and twentieth-century art that so remarkably recreates the Minoan imagery (for example, Toulouse-Lautrec, Matisse, Picasso, Brancusi, and of course the newer ecology art depicting dolphins and other marine life).

Particularly for younger groups or those comfortable with using a creativity exercise, the cofacilitators could in addition bring some modeling clay and/or other artistic materials. This would give the group a chance to experiment with the kinds of forms and images elicited in them by the art of Crete. People love to create, but our society generally relegates creativity to those judged to have "talent."

Remind participants of the readings for the next session. Ask them to look over the suggested Discussion Topics and be prepared to choose those of most interest. If someone does not have *The Partnership Way*, a group member should be asked to share or the facilitators should make and hand out copies of the discussion topics.

Closing

Before closing you might suggest that a celebration of some kind be planned for the next meeting. The celebration could include a potluck meal or the sharing of some special treat (fruits, baked goods, or whatever the group prefers). This sharing could be a symbol for a partnership ritual where both women and men share not only the eating together but also the planning *and* the preparation of the food. Often this is done at the last meeting of a series, and you may prefer to do it this way. However, also doing it at some halfway point is a good way of forming closer group bonds.

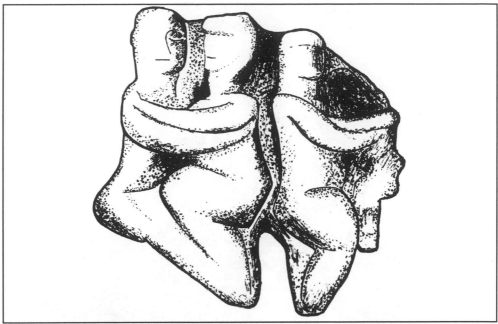

ANCIENT PARTNERS. THIS MAY BE ONE OF THE EARLIEST REPRESENTATIONS OF THE
HIEROS GAMOS, OR "SACRED MARRIAGE." LINKED TOGETHER IN THE ORIGINAL
CARVING IN GREENISH-GRAY STONE, TO THE LEFT WE SEE A COUPLE EMBRACING; TO
THE RIGHT IS THE RESULT OF MOTHER AND CHILD. THIS SCENE OF ANCIENT
PARTNERS DATES BACK TO 6000 B.C. LINE DRAWING BY JIM BEEMAN FROM THE
ORIGINAL.

THIS IS A SKETCH OF A CARVING OF AN ANTELOPE ON A PIECE OF BONE DATING
BACK TO 20,000 B.C. NEXT TO THE ANTELOPE ARE THE "WRONG-WAY ARROWS":
FOR MANY YEARS, AUTHORITIES ROUTINELY IDENTIFIED THESE OBJECTS AS
ARROWS BEING SHOT AT THE ANTELOPE, EVEN THOUGH THESE "ARROWS"
CURIOUSLY SEEM TO BE MISSING THEIR MARK. THROUGH CAREFUL ANALYSIS
ALEXANDER MARSHACK PROVED THESE WERE NOT WEAPONS BUT VEGETATION —
WITH THE BRANCHES GOING THE RIGHT WAY.
LINE DRAWING BY JEFF HELWIG FROM THE ORIGINAL.

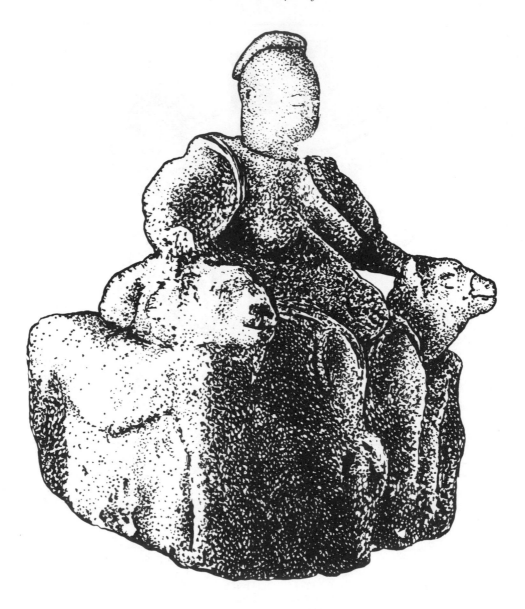

A GODDESS FIGURINE FOUND IN CATAL HUYUK, TURKEY, DATING BACK TO 5750
B.C. SHE IS SEATED ON A THRONE, GIVING BIRTH, WHILE FLANKED BY WHAT ARE
IDENTIFIED BY MOST AUTHORITIES AS TWO LEOPARDS. WHAT IS BELIEVED TO BE
THE TAIL OF ONE OF THE LEOPARDS CAN BE SEEN WRAPPED OVER HER RIGHT
SHOULDER.

Session 4
The Essential Difference

Goals

1. To discover something of the beauty and power of the civilization of Minoan Crete and how it presaged much that we value in ancient Greece and in our own time.

2. To reflect on "the essential difference" that animated the Minoan social order.

3. To begin to explore the ways in which the rediscovery of ancient patterns of possibility can add satisfying and creative new dimensions to our own lives and our own society.

4. To reexamine some of our archetypes of heroes and heroines and their implications for our lives and our planet.

Readings

The Chalice and the Blade
Chapter 3, "The Essential Difference: Crete"

Materials

Regular supplies plus art brought by group members and optional artistic materials (see Session 3's section on preparation for this session).

Preparation for Facilitators

Same as for Session 2. For those groups that have decided to have a potluck this will be a shorter session and facilitators will have to pace it accordingly.

Getting Started

Begin the meeting as before. By now the group will have worked out a comfortable and effective way of starting each session, which serves as a transition from the outside world to a regular time and place for relating and learning in partnership. It could be a short ceremony. It could be listening to a short passage from the audio tape abridgement of *The Chalice and the Blade* by Riane Eisler. It could be a brief meditation.

Ask participants to share what, in the readings and sessions, has been most important or meaningful and most distressing or difficult for them up until now. When appropriate, bring the group to this session's focus, "the essential difference" that was Crete.

To get into the material on Crete, one option is to start by looking at the pictures in the books the cofacilitators and other people have brought. Also, there are many line drawings of Minoan seals and other images in this book that people may want to talk about.

By looking at some of the pictures of Minoan art as well as contemporary art reviving these motifs, we can begin to explore the important question of what kinds of images reinforce partnership rather than dominator ways of thinking and living on this Earth. Even more specifically, we can begin to look at the archetypes we have been taught of women and men, and how we can create for ourselves new partnership heroes and heroines.

We have all been taught dominator ways of thinking and living. And although there are very strong pressures moving us in a partnership direction, much of our culture continues to reinforce the dominator ways.

A good exercise that highlights this and is also fun and creative focuses on the differences between dominator and partnership archetypes. It dramatically shows how heroes and heroines unconsciously give power to the particular roles that are required by either a dominator or partnership system.

In this exercise the participants are asked to work in dyads (in mixed groups, dyads of the same gender). The exercise begins with one of the participants role-playing one of the dominator heroines or heroes for a few minutes, or if that is difficult, at least telling a story about a heroine or hero, or talking about some examples or some of the characteristics that go with this particular archetype.

Dominator Heroines and Heroes

If we look at many of our archetypal models for women, we see that they are appropriate for a dominator society. For example, women have to suffer greatly in such a system. This is why we find so many Suffering Heroines in our stories.

The Suffering Heroine can take a number of forms: She can be the Sacrificing Heroine, such as the selfless mother, daughter, sister, or wife (a very popular heroine in religious and classical stories). She can be the Masochistic Heroine, the woman who derives pleasure from her suffering (a very popular heroine in much of contemporary pornography).

Other heroines model passivity and incompetence. There is the Helpless Heroine, all the way from Sleeping Beauty to the classic cartoon of the woman tied to the railroad tracks, waiting to be rescued by a male hero. Then there is the Foolish Heroine (exemplified by the "dumb blonde"). Also popular are the Deranged Heroine or Romantic Madwoman (such as Ophelia in *Hamlet)*, and the Fallen Woman (who is punished for being "dishonored" by a man), as well as the Dying Heroine (such as in *Love Story),* who often even has to pay with her life for freely choosing whom to love (as in the famous operas *Carmen* and *La Traviata).*

And we are all familiar with the Saintly Heroine (the holy virgin) and the Evil Heroine (going back to Pandora and Eve). These archetypes give power to the idea that unless they are superhuman (above all carnal or worldly desires), women are subhuman and thus must be controlled by men — for their own and everyone else's good. Another variation is the Scheming Heroine who is punished for asserting herself and/or seeking self-expression (such as Alexis in *Dynasty* and the stereotype of the unhappy, unfulfilled career woman).

Dominator heroines have their counterparts in dominator heroes. Along with the sacrificing mother, daughter, sister, or wife, we find the Outstanding Hero (the legendary winner, leader, strong man, or man at the top). Related to him is the Courageous Hero (almost always also a Violent Hero) for whom the Helpless Heroine is the standard foil and/or prize. The Omniscient Hero (the "divinely ordained" king or modern "expert") is a dominator complement to the Foolish Heroine.

The Hero as Warrior is almost always egged on to battle by some version of a passive dominator heroine. And perhaps the most pervasive image associated with masculinity is the archetype of the Lord, the Lord who rules from heaven, as the head of a government, or as the head of a household or lord of the castle that is his home.

After about five minutes, the facilitator signals that it is now time to switch to the other member of the dyad to create a partnership alternative by either telling a story, role playing, or describing an alternative by her or his partner to the particular dominator archetype described.

Partnership Heroines and Heroes

The partnership alternative to the Helpless Heroine is the Adventurous Heroine. In Minoan mythology, she could be a bull-dancer (as in the bull-leaping fresco) or the captain of a ship (as in one of the Minoan seals). Or she could be somebody like the astronaut Sally Ride in real life, the goddess Artemis in Greek mythology, or some of the newer science fiction heroines (from writers like Ursula LeGuin, or even the Sigourney Weaver role in films like *Alien;* however, without their simply stepping into the violent/courageous male role). Or in the sciences, she could be a primatologist like Jane Goodall or Dian Fossey (also played by Weaver in *Gorillas in the Mist*).

The alternative to the Foolish Heroine is the Wise Heroine. One example is the Crone, the ancient Wise Woman archetype now being reclaimed by feminist writers such as Mary Daly. More contemporary examples are the Woman as Counselor, such as the many women who are now in family and psychological counseling fields, and the Wise Mother as an antidote for "Father Knows Best." In science, she could be the Nobel prize-winning biologist Barbara McClintock, who pioneered an empathic, rather than purely objective, research method or psychiatrist Jean Baker Miller, whose work validates the wisdom of "feminine" caring and emphasis on the importance of relationship.

Instead of the Suffering Heroine we can have the Actualizing Heroine. By actualizing both herself and others, this woman shows that you do not have to actualize yourself at the expense of others. Contemporary examples are women artists and actresses who are also political activists such as Judy Chicago and Jane Fonda. Another alternative to the Suffering and/or Dying Heroine is the Happy Heroine who independently and freely chooses how to live and love, following both her heart and her mind.

A good alternative to both the Saintly and the Evil Heroine is the Spiritual Heroine. She can be a priestess of the Goddess such as Ariadne was in Crete. Or she can be a contemporary woman like so many of us today seeking to reclaim our birthright of direct connection to our higher and more spiritually enlightened selves.

An alternative to the Hero as Conqueror is the Hero as Healer. This can be a healer of the body who works in partnership with the person to be healed and does not just "give orders" as we have been taught to see doctors. It can be a man working to heal the Earth as an environmental or peace activist. Or it can be a man organizing groups such as Men Against Rape and other avenues for diagnosing and healing the male's identification with violence in a dominator society. Well-known models of social and spiritual healers in our time are Mahatma Gandhi and Martin Luther King.

An alternative to the archetype of the Hero as Warrior is the Hero as Mediator. As Mark Gerzon writes in *A Choice of Heroes*, "The Mediator does not require that life be a battle, nor does he equate heroism with fighting valorously; rather, the Mediator's heroic calling is to stand between the opposing armies. His goal is to enable the adversaries to coexist, if possible, to cooperate. He is not necessarily a pacifist … he is simply no longer enamored with violence."

The partnership alternative to many of the stereotypical male heroes is the Hero as Nurturer. He can be a tiller of the soil or a fisherman (as in the Minoan fresco from the island of Santorini). He can be a teacher (however, one who does not feign omniscience). He can be a religious leader (but not one who pretends that he has a direct line to God or that because he is a man he is more spiritual than a woman).

In everyday life the Nurturer is the new father who is today emerging, freeing himself of the stereotypes of head of family/provider/king of his castle to explore and express his soft or "feminine" side. As Gerzon writes, "The Nurturer does not conceive children with the belief that someone else must take care of them. He sees himself as responsible for their growth as for their birth…. The Nurturer does not view spending time with his children as doing them or his wife a favor. He considers it a basic part of his life."

Another important alternative to the Macho Man or Hero as Warrior is the Sensitive Hero. This is the man who no longer feels that he has to suppress his feelings of empathy. It is also the "effeminate" or "effete" artistic man (such as the young man walking in a garden in the Minoan fresco, the "starving artist" characteristic of dominator history, or the many young men who are in our time learning that "real" men can — and do — have feelings other than disgust and anger).

Basically, what this exercise helps us do is to imbue with significance or "heroism" roles appropriate to a partnership-oriented culture, one where as in Minoan Crete the most valued role for both women and men is that of the Nurturer, once symbolized by the Great Goddess as the source of "the beauty, the passion, and the truth of love."

Further Exercises

The following exercise can be used in addition to or instead of the preceding one.

Journey to Crete

The cofacilitators ask the group to close their eyes, relax, and take a mental journey to Crete.

Imagine yourself as a woman or man living in Minoan times.

- What kinds of relationships do you form?

- What are your attitudes about sex?

- How are children taken care of and educated?

- How do you think of yourself in relation to nature?

- How do you experience spirituality?

After participants have created a "movie" based on these questions, the facilitators may want them to break into dyads or small groups and share the stories with each other. Then, the group could come back together and share their stories, noting the similarities and differences in the stories and the similarities and differences between their imagined story and their current reality. Encourage people to have fun and be as creative and outrageous as they can. After all, in a fantasy, magical things can happen.

As in every session, the facilitators should use the newsprint pad to record the feelings and ideas shared by the members of the group.

Those groups that feel comfortable with this may also want to tap their own creativity, either at this session or outside, by experimenting with the forms and images elicited in them by the art of Crete.

Discussion Topics

1. What major characteristics distinguished Minoan Crete from other ancient civilizations with which we may be more familiar? What constituted "the essential difference"?

2. Does the changing face of modern life in America, Europe, or elsewhere reflect something genuinely akin to the "Cretan" spirit revealed in the archeological record? If so, what do such changes portend? If not, are apparent parallels only superficial? Consider such areas as:

- art, architecture, literature;

- the social roles of women and men;

- religion, spirituality;

- the "New Age," ecology, peace, women's, and other movements;

- some of the new labyrinthine shopping malls;

- women in sports; and

- androgynous fashions for women and men.

3. What is the role of myth, archetypes, and symbols in establishing and maintaining a cultural paradigm?

- Can you find similarities between the iconography and symbols of this earlier partnership-oriented culture and those emerging in movements focusing on peace, ecology, feminism, etc;?

- Are we living in an age of "mythlessness" (that is; have the central stories and symbols of our culture begun to lose their meaning)?

4. What view of sexuality is reflected in the archeological record of Minoan Crete?

- How does this relate to the modern "sexual revolution" and women's movement?

- What are the social implications of a culture's outlook on sexuality? (The pictures of Minoan women and men are of slim people, with no huge differences in the musculature and size of women and men. We also learn from the bull-dancing fresco and other images that both women and men were athletic. This could lead to an interesting discussion of whether there is a relationship between the current revival of athletics for women and the trend toward a more relaxed and mutually satisfying sex life for both women and men.)

- What in the culture do you think contributed to the Minoans' evident joy in life?

- How do you think they resolved conflict?

- Why do you think they had no fortifications?

- Why do you think "feminine" sensitivity was expressed so vividly in their art?

5. Which sentence or paragraph in the assigned reading is most significant to you? Why?

- In terms of your own life?

- With respect to modern culture?

- In its implications for the human condition?

Supplementary Reading

For full titles and citations, see the References at the end of this book.

Harry Brod, *The Making of Masculinities*

Mary Daly, *Gyn/Ecology*

Riane Eisler, *Sacred Pleasure* (particularly chapters 7 and 8)

Mark Gerzon, *A Choice of Heroes*

Jacquetta Hawkes, *The Dawn of the Gods*

bell hooks, *Feminist Theory: From Margin to Center*

Nikolas Platon, *Crete*

Adrienne Rich, *Of Woman Born*

Karen Signell, *Wisdom of the Heart: Working with Women's Dreams*

Demaris S. Wehr, *Jung and Feminism: Liberating Archetypes*

Preparation for the Next Session

Remind participants of the readings for the next session and, if someone does not have *The Partnership Way,* hand out copies of "The Language of Partnership." Ask people to bring some materials to share that they feel symbolize the shift in our prehistory from a partnership to a dominator model as the main guide in our cultural evolution. This could be art or illustrations in books idealizing destruction and domination, such as scenes of heroic warriors, hallowed conquerors dragging prisoners in chains; or gods like Zeus raping women. Cofacilitators should also be sure to bring some materials themselves, including images of the Goddess as androgynous (like the one on the cover of *The Chalice and the Blade).* Images reflecting female-male complementarity; such as the Minoan Goddess figurines and male horns of consecration (showing the importance of the Bull or Horned God) are also useful and can be found in Platon's *Crete.* These serve as contrast to later images.

Closing

As appropriate.

THE FAMOUS BULL DANCERS FROM A FRESCO AT THE PALACE OF KNOSSOS, CRETE.
PARTICULARLY FASCINATING IS THE FACT THAT THE FIGURE TO THE LEFT HOLDING
THE BULL BY THE HORNS AND THE FIGURE TO THE RIGHT TOSSING THE ACROBAT
ARE FEMALE — TRADITIONALLY DEPICTED AS WHITE IN CRETAN ART.
THE CENTRAL FIGURE — TRADITIONALLY RED IN COLOR — IS MALE.
LINE DRAWING FROM THE ORIGINAL BY JEFF HELWIG.

A GODDESS FIGURINE FROM MINOAN CRETE. DONE IN THE HIGHLY GLAZED CERAMIC TECHNIQUE KNOWN AS FAIENCE, THIS GODDESS IS ONE OF TWO SIMILARLY BARE-BREASTED "SNAKE GODDESSES" DATING BACK TO 1600 B.C. HOLDING SNAKES IN BOTH HANDS, SHE ALSO HAS A CAT SITTING ON TOP OF HER HEAD. FELINES WERE THE SYMBOL OF THE GODDESS AND HER PRIESTESSES. HENCE, AFTER THE DOMINATOR SHIFT, IN KEEPING WITH THE DRIVE TO WHOLLY DISCREDIT THE EARLIER WAYS, WE FIND THE CAT NOW ASSOCIATED WITH EVIL AND THE MEDIEVAL "WITCH." LINE DRAWING BY JOHN MASON FROM THE ORIGINAL.

TYPICAL OF MINOAN CRETE IS THIS PREMILITARISTIC, PRE-MACHO PORTRAYAL OF THE "NATURAL" MALE. RATHER THAN BEING FORCED TO ARMOR HIMSELF TO DO BATTLE IN THE WORLD, HE CAN CONCENTRATE ON SOMETHING THAT MAKES MORE SENSE — BEING A FISHERMAN AND FOOD PROVIDER. FROM A FRESCO IN MINOAN THERA, ABOUT 1500 B.C.. LINE DRAWING BY JIM BEEMAN FROM THE ORIGINAL.

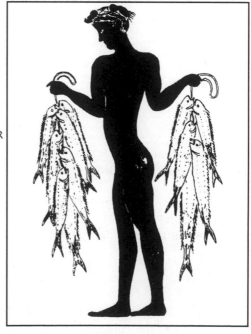

Session 5
The Interruption of Civilization

Goals

1. To reexamine the common assumption that prehistoric societies were primitive, matriarchal, and uncivilized, and that warfare, male dominance, and slavery are necessary characteristics of civilization.

2. To reflect on the degree to which these assumptions continue to influence our lives today.

3. To inquire more deeply into prevailing models of power, spirituality, and nature, and their personal and social consequences.

4. To begin to explore how the suggestion that a major cultural shift, a radical transformation in world view or paradigm that occurred in the ancient world, relates to the possibility that another such transformation may be under way today.

Readings

The Chalice and the Blade:
> Chapter 4, "Dark Order Out of Chaos: From the Chalice to the Blade" Figures 6, 7, 8, and 9
> Chapter 5, "Memories of a Lost Age: The Legacy of the Goddess"

The Partnership Way:
> "The Language of Partnership" in Partnership Resources.

Materials

Regular supplies plus art brought by group members and cofacilitators (see Session 4's section on preparation for this session).

Preparation for Facilitators

Same as for Session 2.

The Victorian fantasy *Flatland* by Edwin Abbott also provides an excellent approach to the discussion of paradigm shift as the transformation of a culture's fundamental values and assumptions. A useful excerpt from this work can be found in Marilyn Ferguson's *The Aquarian Conspiracy*, pp. 65-66. Facilitators may want to bring copies for handouts.

Getting Started

Begin the meeting as usual. You may want to begin by reading the following note from Riane Eisler:

> "When I wrote *The Chalice and the Blade*, I was acutely, often very painfully, aware of how our Goddess heritage has been denied us in conventional religious and secular accounts, and how very difficult it therefore is for us to imagine a female deity. This is why Chapter 5 is subtitled 'The Legacy of the Goddess' and focuses on the Goddess and on women. But I think it is important to remember that there are also ancient male symbols of divinity, such as the many bucrania (bull horns) in Catal Huyuk shrines and the horns of consecration in Knossos and other Minoan sites.
>
> As noted in *The Chalice and the Blade*, the bull seems to have represented the male life force. And the emphasis on the horned and hoofed animals in 20,000-year-old European caves could indicate that this symbology goes back all the way to the Paleolithic, where we often find paintings of animal pairs, female and male. In other words, just as the 'Venus' figurines prefigure the Great Goddess as the giver and nurturer of life, the Bull God (later discredited as the Devil) may also have very ancient roots.
>
> I am adding these lines to again emphasize something that is, of course, an underlying theme in *The Chalice and the Blade* and my other works. This is that while the power to give and sustain life was conceptualized in female form (after all, life emerges from the female body), the male was also honored (and revered).
>
> In short, while the Great Goddess was revered as the Mother of all Nature and Life, these were gender-balanced or partnership-oriented societies. Men, as well as women, played important roles. The critical difference is that, in contrast to dominator-oriented societies, here the male role and 'masculinity' were *not* equated with domination and conquest, be it of women, other men, or nature."

Either preceding or following the reading of this note by Riane Eisler, facilitators could play a short excerpt from the audio tape where she reads from *The Chalice and the Blade*. In fact, facilitators could select appropriate passages to play for each session.

When the group is ready, facilitators should bring the group to this session's focus, the interruption of civilization. They can use the following exercise to lead this off.

Living in a Great Goddess World

Ask the group to divide into dyads and then close their eyes, relax, and begin to imagine that they are living in a world that worships a Great Goddess, the Mother of all Nature and Life. (The pictures suggested in preparation for this session could also be helpful here.)

Facilitators can use the following questions like a guided imagery (with some modification), or the questions can be put on newsprint and the group can read them together prior to doing the exercise.

- What does thinking of the Earth as our Mother feel like?

- What kinds of attitudes toward nature come with a belief system centering on a female deity representing creativity and the life-giving and regenerating powers of the universe? (Would "man's conquest of nature" be acceptable in such a society? How about man's conquest and domination of women?)

- What do you think your parents' relationship would have been like in this society where the Great Goddess had both divine sons and daughters?

- How would it have been different from the way it actually was? How would it have been the same?

- How would it have affected the way they felt and acted toward their children? Toward you as their daughter or as their son?

- How would it have affected their attitudes about war? About power? About women's and men's work? About what is moral and immoral? About different races and religions?

- How would it be reflected in language?

Further Exercises

After the opening exercise has been processed, you can use the following additional exercise.

Childhood in a Great Goddess World

Ask participants to imagine themselves as children in a society where a Great Goddess is worshiped — where in their homes, schools, and places of worship they learn many stories about this divine Mother and her divine daughters and sons.

Or ask them to imagine themselves as children in their own communities today sitting in a church, synagogue, or mosque worshiping a divine Mother and Father whose presence is manifested in all aspects of life and nature, whose love is our birthright as women and men. Also imagine that services are lead by both priestesses and priests.

Pose these questions:

- What is this like for you? How does it make you feel?

- How does it affect your attitudes about yourself? About women? About men? About nature? About power?

- How does it affect our language?

- How does it affect our views about what is normal and proper or ridiculous and unacceptable?

Discussion Topics

1. Discuss how you think your family life has been affected by growing up in a world where men and "masculinity" were valued over women and "femininity" — as in the contempt men often feel for "women's work."

- How do you think your generation is different from that of your parents?

- What changes do you see in the next generation?

Wherever possible, the discussion should be placed in the larger context of a major contemporary cultural shift — this time from domination to partnership as the guiding social image.

2. Discuss why the subordination of women and the feminine is so important in a dominator system.

- How do you think sayings such as "If rape is inevitable, relax and enjoy it" or "All's fair in love and war" developed?

- How do you think the subordination of women relates to racism and other ways of ranking one kind of human being over another based on inborn differences?

- How do you think war and the "war of the sexes" are related?

- Is world peace possible as long as the so-called hard or masculine values of conquest and domination are idealized?

3. How are racism, antisemitism, and other discriminatory isms related to the dominator model?

- What are your thoughts about the suggestion made by the cultural historian Merlin Stone that racism was brought by the Indo-European invasions since the darker skinned Dravidians (the earlier inhabitants of India) became the "untouchable" Indian lowest caste after the Indo-Europeans took over?

- How do you think intertribal violence relates to the dominator model?

- How do you think the rallying cry "women must be returned to their traditional place in the traditional family" of Hitler's Germany and Khomeini's Iran relates to these regimes' persecution of out-groups such as Jews, Baha'is, and members of minority Muslim sects?

- How do you think the fanning of anti-black sentiments by white supremacists who also preach male control in families and the fanning of antisemitism by some African Americans who also believe in the rightness of male controlled families are related?

- What changes in family structure, gender relations, religious beliefs, and economic institutions do you think can help accelerate racial and multicultural equity?

4. How are our views about power, spirituality, and nature colored by the images, alternatively, of a male ruler of the universe like Jehovah or Zeus (who sits on a throne high above us and wields a thunderbolt or sword) or a Goddess whose body is a Universal Womb and whose symbols are trees, animals, and other aspects of nature?

- To what degree do you or don't you have difficulty with the idea of a female deity? Why?

- How does *The Chalice and the Blade* throw a different light on the story of the Garden of Eden and the legend of Atlantis?

- Why do you suppose the gifts of civilization — the most fundamental of our technological and social inventions — arose from earlier Goddess/partnership cultures?

- What would this kind of system have to do with basic creativity — for example, the invention of language, government, art, and law?

5. How would you describe the role of warfare in instituting and preserving domination and how does it relate to the definition of power as power over rather than power to or with? (You might find Jean Baker Miller's *Toward a New Psychology of Women* particularly helpful in defining different types of power. If groups engage in power exercises or simply list their understandings of what power is, they will come up with a mix of "power-over" and "power-for" ideas. Then the discussion can point out the difference. Again, the ideas come first from the experience of the participants. What is important is to see the implications of different definitions of power by looking at ancient society and then at our own.)

6. Discuss how language reflects and reinforces a dominator or partnership world view, and what changes in our language might dramatically alter the way we view the world.

Supplementary Readings

For full titles and citations, see the References at the end of this book.

Edwin Abbott, *Flatland*

Roy Chamberlin and Herman Feldman, eds., *The Dartmouth Bible*

Riane Eisler, *Sacred Pleasure*

Johan Galtung and Sohail Inayatullah, eds., *Macrohistory and Macrohistorians*

Marija Gimbutas, *The Early Civilization of Europe*

Samuel Noah Kramer and John Maier, *Myths of Enki, the Crafty God*

Min Jaiyin, *The Chalice and the Blade in Chinese Culture*

J. V. Luce, *The End of Atlantis*

Casey Miller and Kate Swift, eds., *Words and Women*

Erich Neumann, *The Great Mother*

Elisabeth Sahtouris, *Gaia: The Human Journey from Chaos to Cosmos*

Merlin Stone, *When God Was a Woman*

Nancy Tanner, *On Becoming Human*

Preparation for the Next Session

Remind the members of the group of the readings for the next session. Ask them to bring one or two examples of what they feel could be typical dominator and, by contrast, partnership art.

Closing

As appropriate.

WARRIORS FROM AN ANCIENT ROMAN MOSAIC. THESE FIGURES VIVIDLY SHOW
THE CONTRAST BETWEEN THE EARLIER, MORE PARTNERSHIP-ORIENTED ART AND
THE EMPHASIS ON CONFLICT, DEATH, AND PAIN THAT FOLLOW WITH THE
IMPOSITION OF THE DOMINATOR MODEL. IN THE ORIGINAL, THE FIGURE SHOWN
VERTICAL HERE IS HORIZONTAL, HAVING FALLEN, THE OTHER ABOUT TO KILL HIM.
WE HAVE TURNED THE FIGURES THIS WAY BECAUSE OF THE STRANGE "DANCE OF
DEATH" EFFECT.

THE MURDER OF PENTHESILEA BY ACHILLES, FROM AN ATHENIAN AMPHORA, OR
VASE, PRIOR TO THE FIFTH CENTURY B.C. ONE OF HUNDREDS OF THOUSANDS OF
PRECURSORS OF OUR MOVIE AND TV KILLINGS, THIS WAS DONE IN THE MEDIUM OF
THAT TIME, POTTERY, IN THE BLACK FIGURE TECHNIQUE, WHERE FOR GREATER
IMPACT THE BLACK FIGURE IS SILHOUETTED AGAINST THE RED GROUND OF THE POT.
LINE DRAWING BY JOHN MASON FROM THE ORIGINAL.

Session 6
The Great Cover-Up

Goals

1. To begin to reassess conventional assumptions about morality, knowledge, and truth in light of the information examined in the preceding readings and sessions.

2. To relate this information to our own life experiences, particularly with respect to issues of control.

3. To reexamine our assumptions about reality, particularly in relation to the almost exclusive conventional focus in our schools and universities on the experiences and ideas of men.

Readings

The Chalice and the Blade:
    Chapter 6, "Reality Stood on its Head: Part I"
    Chapter 7, "Reality Stood on its Head: Part II"

Materials

Regular supplies plus art brought by group members (see Session 5's section on preparation for this session).

Preparation for Facilitators

Same as for Session 2.

Getting Started

The facilitators could begin by reading or telling an ancient story reflecting the remything process that so profoundly altered our perception of reality during the shift to a warlike, male-dominant, authoritarian society. For example, there are many myths of the old goddesses or their sons battling the new warrior gods, and having power forcibly taken from them. But there are also myths of the old goddesses marrying the new gods or being persuaded or tricked to hand over their power.

These myths are pertinent today. Women do not always battle openly because the conflict is often covert. Or if they do assert power openly, they often find themselves in trouble. On the other hand, men (who are in male-dominant societies supposed to have a monopoly on power), are also tricked into believing they can always be in control. In fact, much of their lives is directly controlled by other men who are their "superiors," and they are also many times manipulated by "inferiors" such as women.

Getting groups to engage in discussions of how women and men have personal power taken from them or allow themselves to be tricked into giving it away might be a way to begin examining more closely the interplay of partnership and dominator models in our personal lives.

The whole issue of control (of self and others) versus trust also directly leads back to the basic question of how we define power: as power over or power to and with. It further leads to the whole question of myths about the roles of women and men and the realization that attempts to maintain superiority or dominance are inimical to any really satisfying or partnership relationship.

Further Exercises

Those groups that wish to do more experiential work may decide to use the following provocative guided visualization, which is adapted in part from a role-reversal exercise developed by Theodora Wells.

The Flip-Flop World

Ask the participants to relax in the usual way. Then explain that this guided visualization is intended not only to help us experience a gender role reversal, but also to gain insight into what it might have been like to have one's whole world view literally stood on its head through new and very different stories and myths about what is human nature and/or divinely ordained.

It is very important to stress that the purpose of this visualization is to help us feel how profoundly myths shape our view of ourselves and of what we consider reality. On one level, this exercise is a way of raising awareness about the arbitrary nature of some of our most hallowed assumptions. On another, and even more important level, it makes it possible for us to see that matriarchy is indeed the other side of the coin of the dominator model, and that a very different type of mythology has to be constructed to support a partnership society.

Ask the participants to close their eyes and go back to their childhoods and imagine that they have been born into and have grown up in a world where the following realities exist.

- Practically every time one picks up the newspaper or turns on the TV to find out what the world's leaders are doing, the pictures and names are those of women.

- When top religious leaders speak or write, they are usually women talking or writing about what women popes, bishops, and spiritual leaders have done or are doing.

- The prevailing view of the nature of women and men stresses that there are obvious biological explanations for women's leadership. Women are the life-givers, and their bodies are the incarnation of life-giving and life-sustaining power. Moreover, female genitals are compact and internal, protected by the body, while male genitals are external and exposed. Hence women are naturally meant to be the protectors of men, whose activities must be controlled for their own good and the good of the race, lest their reproductive vulnerability threaten the continuity of the human race.

- It is widely believed that in sexual intercourse the male genitals are engulfed by the protective body of the woman.

- Males yearn for this protection, fully realizing their masculinity at this time — or a man only experiences himself as a "whole man" when thus engulfed. If a male denies these feelings, he is unconsciously denying his masculinity.

- Women are not only protective and controlling of men; they also must exclude them from dangerous and unsuitable activities. Sometimes this may seem cruel, as when a boy's sisters jeer at him when he runs or climbs because his primitive genitals flap around foolishly. But while girls can develop their bodies and minds freely in preparation for the active responsibilities of womanhood, males must be taught to be less active. Moreover, sheltering men in the homemaking virtues is both moral and natural, as in this way the males' passive nurturing role in the family balances the biological contribution of the woman to the race through pregnancy and childbirth.

- The superiority of women is also reflected in the language, where woman and womankind are generic terms that quite literally include man in them. Books, movies, plays, and courses of all kinds are thus called "The Story of

Woman" or "The Study of Woman" — as everyone knows this also includes men.

Ask the participants to imagine that it has always been this way, every day of our lives. Ask them to feel what it would be like being born into such a world, growing up in it (either as girls or boys), becoming adults, experiencing what it means to be a woman or a man.

Ask them also to imagine what would happen once men found out this had not always been so — and all the pressure there would be to suppress this information.

Finally, ask them to imagine what could be done to make this a more balanced partnership world: particularly what kinds of stories and images could help such a change, how morality, good, and evil could be redefined, how women's and men's roles could be redefined in a way conducive to equal partnership rather than one-sided control and domination.

Then ask the group to share these ideas, feelings, and blueprints for a more balanced partnership future and, as always, note these on the newsprint pad.

Discussion Topics

1. Discuss more recent attempts to rewrite history and compare them to the remything that took place in our prehistory.

- Do the Stalin era, the McCarthy hearings, or more recently, the activities and pronouncements of groups like the Moral Majority reveal similar dynamics? What about Khomeini's "Islamic Revolution" in Iran and the teaching that women are dangerous and must be controlled for their own good and the good of the society?

- What kinds of myths have been most significant in imposing and maintaining male dominance and authoritarianism?

- What message about human nature is imparted by the Adam and Eve and Cain and Abel stories? About the "inevitability" of war and the war of the sexes? About "man's innate violence"? About how men, and especially women, have to be controlled "for their own good"?

- After reading Chapter 7, what are your thoughts about the relation between politics, economics, and codes of morality? What are your feelings about the story of Lot and other biblical accounts where "moral" men directly or indirectly abuse and even murder women and children?

- Many religions seem to believe and teach that human suffering and injustice are inevitable, even holy. How do you think this belief system perpetuates a dominator society? What kind of belief system do you think a partnership society would have to explain human suffering and injustice? How would it be different?

2. What new insights can we bring to bear on the study of religious and secular classics that idealize the dominator system (for example, passages in Greek literature, in the Bible, or even in the works of Shakespeare that idealize armed conquest and male dominance)?

- Should the classroom presentation and discussion of such materials be changed? If so, how?

- What are the implications of the challenge to the dominator model for the established religious traditions? Is a transformation of existing religious patterns and structures likely or possible?

3. How do you think the reassessment in recent years of the treatment of American Indians in the teaching of U.S. history relates to the reassessment of prehistoric societies formerly described as "primitive," "barbarian," and not worthy of study?

- How does the teaching to children that Native Americans were an obstacle to the "civilizing" of the West relate to the notion that the Indo-European invaders of Europe were the first civilized people in Europe?

- How have stereotypes of Indians as violent barbarians served to justify the breaking of treaties and massacres of Indians?

- What can we today learn from Native American traditions about harmony with nature?

- How do you think this traditional wisdom relates to the images of Grandmother of the Corn, Spider Woman, and other positive images of powerful spiritual female deities in American Indian traditions?

4. How can the information now being gathered by feminist scholars and others about the past and present of the ignored female half of humanity be integrated into our schools and universities?

5. Some people think that the advent and elaboration of the patriarchal and dominator motifs came about because of a deliberate cover-up of the ancient order and an effort to hide the truth. Some people think that it was not so much a matter of a deliberate attempt to hide the truth, but rather the ancient order was suppressed by those who failed to recognize its value. What do you think?

6. What are the consequences of identifying children exclusively by the surname of the father? Sharon Lebell's book *Naming Ourselves, Naming Our Children* deals with this issue. It raises questions like the following:

- Should children bear their mother's and father's names — and in which order?

- Should they select their own names?

- How practical are alternatives to present custom?

7. What other feelings, thoughts, and memories have been evoked by reading these chapters and discussing the questions?

Supplementary Readings

For full titles and citations, see the References at the end of this book.

Anne Llewellyn Barstow, *Witchcraze: A New History of the European Witch Hunts*

Kathleen Barry, *Female Sexual Slavery*

Matthew Callahan, *Sex, Death, and the Angry Young Man: Conversations with Riane Eisler and David Loye*

Roy Chamberlin and Herman Feldman, eds., *The Dartmouth Bible*

Carol Christ and Judith Plaskow, eds., *Womanspirit Rising*

Scott Coltrane, "Father-Child Relations and the Status of Women: A Cross-Cultural Study"

Mary Daly, *Gyn/Ecology*

Riane Eisler, *Sacred Pleasure*

Anne Fausto-Sterling, *Myths of Gender: Biological Theories about Women and Men*

Kay Leigh Hagen, ed., *Women Respond to the Men's Movement*

bel hooks, *Feminist Theory: From Margin to Center*

Sharon Lebell, *Naming Ourselves, Naming Our Children*

George Orwell, *1984*

Raphael Patai, *The Hebrew Goddess*

Joan Rockwell, *Fact in Fiction*

Rosemary Radford Ruether, ed., *Religion and Sexism*

Christine E. Sleeter, *Multicultural Education as Social Activism*

Elizabeth Cady Stanton, *The Woman's Bible*

Preparation for the Next Session

Remind participants of the readings for the next session. Ask them to think particularly about goals 1 to 3 for Session 7 and to keep these in mind as they do the assigned readings and as they observe the week's news and events in their own lives during the week.

Closing

As appropriate.

THE GODDESS ATHENA. WHAT HAS HAPPENED TO THE GODDESS DURING THE HYBRIDIZATION OF THE DOMINATOR SHIFT IS INDICATED BY THE SERPENT AND VEGITATION OF HER OLD ALLIANCE ON ONE SIDE, AND THE SPEAR AND THE SHIELD OF THE NEW REGIME, ON THE OTHER. THIS FIGURE WAS CARVED INTO A TINY PERSONAL SEAL IN CARNELIAN, FOUND IN CYPRUS, DATING TO THE FIFTH CENTURY B.C.
LINE DRAWING BY JOHN MASON FROM THE ORIGINAL.

ADAM AND EVE BEING EXPELLED FROM THE GARDEN OF EDEN, FROM THE FRESCO EXPULSION OF ADAM AND EVE FROM PARADISE (C. 1425) BY THE BRILLIANT RENAISSANCE PAINTER MASACCIO (1401-1428). IN THIS ENGRAVING, EVE, ASHAMED OF HER BODY AND CLEARLY WITH LOW SELF-ESTEEM, CONTRASTS POIGNANTLY WITH THE SELF-ASSURED, BARE-BREASTED WOMEN OF MINOAN CRETE.
LINE DRAWING BY JOHN MASON FROM THE ORIGINAL.

Session 7
The Quest for Peace, Creativity, and Partnership

Goals

1. To take a fresh look at recorded history from a new perspective taking into account both halves of humanity (women and men) as well as the latest archeological discoveries about prehistoric societies such as Old Europe and Minoan Crete.

2. To reassess ideals and realities of democracy in ancient Greece and in the modern world from the perspective of the dominator and partnership models.

3. To gain new insights into Christianity — as it began and as it developed — from the consideration of the partnership-dominator dynamic.

4. To begin to allow ourselves to experience our own feelings of loss, anger, and grief, specifically in relation to our hidden partnership heritage and the way powerful stories and images have served to program our subconscious minds, often literally standing reality on its head.

Readings

The Chalice and the Blade:
> Chapter 8, "The Other Half of History: Part I"
> Chapter 9, "The Other Half of History: Part II"
> Chapter 10, "The Patterns of the Past: Gylany and History."

Materials

Regular supplies (see Session 6's section on preparation for this session).

Preparation for Facilitators

Same as for Session 2.

Getting Started

After opening the meeting as usual, you may want to proceed to a discussion of the insights members have had since the last meeting through their experiences and through the readings for this session.

Ask each person to share an insight that relates specifically to goals 2 and 3 for this session: a new understanding of democracy and/or Christianity.

For example, the story by Augustine recounted on p. 114 in *The Chalice and the Blade* tells of how when Greek society shifted to descent traced through the father rather than the mother, Athenian women lost the right to vote. This casts a new light on the commonly held idea that Athens was the cradle of democracy. This in turn has interesting ramifications for the understanding of modern developments, such as the contemporary struggle of women for equal political rights and participation.

Another specific point is the new understanding we gain of prayer to the Catholic Virgin Mary as a reflection and also a co-option of prayer to the ancient Goddess. Again, the fact that "Mariology" came out of a period of strong gylanic resurgence (see Chapter 10 of *The Chalice and the Blade)* makes it easier to see how the contemporary surge of interest in the Goddess and the struggle of women to reenter the priesthood relates to the powerful contemporary partnership thrust.

You may want to imagine yourselves in an early Christian community where the deity was described as both Mother and Father and both women and men were leaders. You may also want to imagine what kinds of prayers were said. You could make up such a prayer or the key elements in it, perhaps beginning with "Our Holy Mother and Father, in thy love we trust."

Further Exercises

At this point some members of the group might want to express their grief and/or anger about all that was lost in the shift from a partnership to a dominator direction, or to find some way to honor that heritage. One way of doing this is to ask the group to try to create a ritual in celebration of the Goddess or for personal healing.

A Healing Ritual

Vicki Noble's *Motherpeace,* Hallie Austin Iglehart's *Womanspirit,* and Starhawk's *The Spiral Dance* are useful sources of information on creating rituals. You might want to start with an invocation from Starhawk's adaptation of "Charge of the Star Goddess":

"I who am the beauty of the green earth and the white moon among the stars and the mysteries of the waters, I call upon your soul to arise and come unto Me. For I am the soul of Nature that gives life to the universe. From Me all things proceed and unto Me they must return. Let My worship be in the heart that rejoices, for behold — all acts of love and pleasure are my rituals."

Then the participants might want to share their feelings. Ask them to particularly comment on how it feels to have both women and men prepare and officiate at a ritual, rather than just having it done by men.

Living in a world where the focus is on only half of humanity — where women (or if it were a matriarchy, men) are by and large written out of what is considered important knowledge or information — is like walking around with blinders on. Use the following exercise to treat this subject more lightly.

A Half-World Exercise

Have the participants cover their eyes with one hand, leaving only a slight crack between two fingers over one eye to peer through.

Discuss the difference in what you see. Then walk around the room, trying to avoid bumping into one another. Report how soon you begin to adapt to this distortion — how soon you can perform adequately with an incomplete information base. Now take your hand away. How is our perception of reality distorted by limited perceptual input?

As in every session, the facilitators should use the newsprint pad to record the feelings and ideas shared by the members of the group.

Discussion Topics

1. The terms *androcracy* and *gylany* are used to describe two different "attractors" affecting the dialectical movement between periods of greater creativity, peace, and equity on the one hand and times of heightened male dominance, repression, and warfare on the other.

- What are the implications of this periodic wave pattern for our present and future?

- How does looking at both halves of humanity (women and men) and the values stereotypically attributed to "femininity" and "masculinity" help us see the connections between:

- rigid male dominance and war?

- the patriarchal family structure and an authoritarian government?

- a partnership family and real democracy?

2. Our primarily Western heritage is said to derive from ancient Greece and the Judeo-Christian tradition. Today, an even more ancient heritage is becoming apparent. Discuss the implications of these discoveries.

In relation to ancient Greece, for example:

- It has been suggested that the *Odyssey*, partly because it contains so many portraits of powerful female figures, was written by a woman. Do you think there may be merit to this theory? What elements of the *Odyssey* do you think reflect the author's wish to honor the earlier heritage where women were priestesses and practiced the esoteric arts of healing and magic? What parts of the *Odyssey* reflect the need in an already primarily dominator society to tell a story where only male warriors can be heroes? Could the author have been deliberately trying to sneak in some of the earlier mythology? Or could it have been primarily unconscious?

- Explore possible connections between Catal Huyuk, Minoan Crete, and pre-Socratic Greece. What may link the three in terms of geography and settlement? In terms of belief systems and values? What is different?

- Discuss the most compelling evidence of the mix of partnership and dominator cultures in ancient Greece. What are some elements of partnership culture? What are some elements of dominator culture?

- What do you think of Aristophanes' satirical portrayal of an early women's peace movement in *Lysistrata?* If you are familiar with the play, you may want to discuss the use of trivialization and humor at the expense of women and compare with sexist, black, or other ethnic jokes.

In relation to Christianity, the following questions may be of interest:

- What do you think your reaction would be if the teachings about compassion, empathy (doing unto others as you would want them to do unto you), and nonviolence (turning the other cheek) attributed to Jesus were instead attributed to a woman? What would be your first reaction? How do you think others would react — all the way from prominent political and religious leaders to your neighbors?

- Consider the question of whether Mary Magdalene was really a prostitute. In the first printing of *The Chalice and the Blade* that was assumed, on the basis of the New Testament. But there is also the possibility that this was a strategic device for discrediting her as an important Christian leader (which we know she was from the "heretic" Gnostic gospels). Discuss the question of prostitution and whether it would exist in a society where sexual morality did not have a double standard for women and men. (It is interesting to note in this connection that Jesus' arrest seems to have been set up by his stopping the stoning to death of an "immoral" woman; and how he challenged the double standard by asking who was so faultless that he could cast the first stone.)

- Can you remember when you first noticed the contradictions between, on the one hand, what Jesus said and his life and, on the other hand, some of the teachings and practices of the organized Church and professed Christians? How did this recognition affect you? How long did it last? Were you given, or did you find, reasons to quickly overlook this contradiction?

- How are the persecution, death, and vilification of Hypatia (and the canonization of the man who instigated her killing) as well as the witch-hunts and burnings of millions of women (many of them healers and "wise women") paralleled by Moslem fundamentalists' torturing, raping, and killing "errant" women in Iran today (sometimes just women who dared to be unveiled)? How are they related to the burning of family planning clinics by Christian fundamentalists and other acts of violence against women in the United States today?

3.   How do you think education can help us move towards peace, creativity, and partnership?

- When children are taught to memorize the dates of wars rather than the dates of important social reforms, such as laws requiring safe working conditions and prohibiting child labor, what kinds of values does that teach?

- Why do you think the existing curriculum gives so little attention to the Seneca Falls Convention that launched the 19th century feminist movement in 1848?

- Do you think a gender-balanced curriculum that gives equal value to both halves of humanity and to work and qualities stereotypically considered feminine, such as caring for children and nonviolence, is an important part of partnership education?

- Do you think a multicultural curriculum is important to help accelerate the movement to a partnership world? (Riane Eisler's books *Tomorrow's Children* and *Learning for Living* are useful resources here).

Supplementary Readings

For full titles and citations, see the References at the end of this book.

Aristophanes, *Lysistrata*

Mary Beard, *Woman as a Force in History*

Elise Boulding, *The Underside of History*

Roy Chamberlin and Herman Feldman, eds., *The Dartmouth Bible*

Carol Christ and Judith Plaskow, *Womanspirit Rising*

Riane Eisler, *Sacred Pleasure*

Riane Eisler, *Tomorrow's Children*

Riane Eisler, *Learning for Living*

Elisabeth Schüssler Fiorenza, *In Memory of Her*

Carol Gilligan, *In a Different Voice*

Edward Hussey, *The Pre-Socratics*

Ervin Laszlo, *Evolution*

David Loye and Riane Eisler, "Chaos and Transformation"

Kate Millett, *Sexual Politics*

Virginia Ramey Mollenkott, *Women, Men, and the Bible*

Elaine Pagels, *The Gnostic Gospels*

Plato, *The Republic*

John Mansley Robinson, *An Introduction to Early Greek Philosophers*

Betty and Theodore Roszak, "The Hard and the Soft"

Sappho, *Lyrics in the Original Greek*

G. Rattray Taylor, *Sex in History*

Monique Wittig, *Les Guerilleres*

Preparation for the Next Session

Remind group members of the readings for the next session. Again, for those who do not have *The Partnership Way,* facilitators may need to hand out copies of "Seven Basic ... Differences" (pages 165-166, "The Everyday Partnership Action Chart" (pages 172-173) and "Human Rights" (website document). Also, facilitators should put the "Seven ... Differences" on newsprint to put up at the next session.

Closing

As appropriate.

THE TRANSFORMATION OF THE GREAT GODDESS OVER TIME INTO MARY, MOTHER OF JESUS. THIS MADONNA AND CHILD, KNOWN AS THE "VIERGE OUVRANTE," WAS OF PAINTED WOOD, FROM 15TH CENTURY FRANCE. THIS IS THE FIGURE CLOSED. ITS FRONT IS SEGMENTED INTO TWO DOORS. TO PROVIDE AN INTERESTING LEAP AHEAD IN TIME, THESE DOORS OPEN TO REVEAL A SMALLER SCENE OF THE LATER CRUCIFIXION OF THE MAN JESUS SHOWN HERE AS THE CHILD IN HIS MOTHER'S ARMS.
LINE DRAWING BY JOHN MASON FROM THE ORIGINAL.

FROM A MEDIEVAL WOODCUT, 1555 A.D., SHOWING THE BURNING OF THREE WITCHES. THE STRANGE FIGURE AT THE TOP OF THE PICTURE IS IDENTIFIED AS THAT OF THE DEVIL CLAIMING THEIR SOULS. PARTICULARLY INTERESTING IS THE FACT THAT THIS DEVIL HAS BREASTS AND A SERPENTINE BODY. AGAIN WE FIND ART USED TO SELL AND REINFORCE THE IDEA OF WOMEN AS EVIL, AND SUBLIMINALLY — SINCE THE SNAKE WAS ONE OF HER EPIPHANIES — TO VILIFY AND DISCREDIT THE ANCIENT GODDESS.

Session 8
Breaking Free

Goals

1. To examine the modern progressive movements from a new perspective — without separating "women's rights" from "human rights."

2. To examine the relationship between the "private sphere" of the family and the "public" or political world.

3. To review and consolidate our understanding of the six major elements of the partnership and the dominator systems and how these six elements affect our ability to develop creative win/win rather than win/lose (more often, in fact, lose/lose) solutions to problems.

| Six Contrasts Between the Dominator and Partnership Systems ||
Dominator System	Partnership System
Rigid male dominance in all areas of life (as well as stereotypically "hard" or "masculine" social priorities).	Equal partnership between women and men in all areas of life (as well as elevation of stereotypically "soft" or "feminine" values in social governance).
"Strong man" rule, or a generally hierarchic and authoritarian family and social structure (where obedience to orders is expected).	A more democratic and equalitarian family and social structure (where participatory decision making is expected).
A high degree of institutionalized social violence (i.e., rape, wife beating, child abuse, war), that is required to impose and maintain rigid economic, social, and political rankings.	More peaceful and mutually satisfying personal, community, and global relations based on interconnection (linking rather than ranking).
Emphasis on technologies of destruction and domination.	Emphasis on creative technologies that sustain and enhance life.
Conquest of nature.	Respect for nature.
Fear and scarcity as the primary motivators for work.	Stimulation of creativity, self development, group or team responsibility, and concern for the larger community (from local to planetary) as primary motivators for work.

Materials

Regular supplies.

Preparation for Facilitators

Same as for Session 2.

Readings

The Chalice and the Blade:
    Chapter 11, "Breaking Free: The Unfinished Transformation."
The Partnership Way:
    Riane Eisler, "Human Rights: Toward an Integrated Theory for Action"
    "The Partnership and Dominator Models" (Basic Configuration and How to Recognize Them)
    "The Everyday Partnership Action Chart"

Getting Started

This session takes us squarely into present time, into our modern world and the crises and opportunities we face. It focuses on creative partnership alternatives to the dominator model.

After the usual opening, you may want to start by putting up the six major elements of the partnership and dominator systems on newsprint for discussion and review.

Further Exercises

The following exercise relates to "The Partnership and Dominator Models" on pages 163-164 in the Partnership Resources.

From Domination to Partnership

In this exercise, the session facilitator divides a large page of newsprint into three columns, headed "The Dominator Way," at the top of the left column, "The Partnership Way," at the top of the middle column, and "Action," at the top of the right column.

The participants are asked to give examples of contrasting dominator and partnership characteristics, attitudes, and behaviors in all aspects of life, from political and work relations to woman-man relations and child rearing. Then participants are asked to give examples from their own experience, observation, and/or creative thinking of specific ways to shift from the dominator to the partnership model. See the "Everyday Partnership Action Chart" in Partnership Resources for examples to get the group started.

During this exercise, keep the following in mind:

- Try to avoid slipping into a polemical ("us against them") stance and to remind ourselves that we have all learned dominator behaviors, that we are all to varying degrees still conditioned by a world that is oriented more to the dominator than to the partnership model.

- Point out that a partnership society is not a society devoid of conflict. As is brought out in Chapter 13 of *The Chalice and the Blade,* the dominator system *suppresses* conflict — even though conflict is natural since people have different needs, desires, and aspirations. By contrast, the partnership system recognizes conflict and does not suppress it (so that it does not have to take recourse to violence and other extremes). Rather, it deals with conflict creatively, and trains both women and men to do this (this is exemplified by the current trend toward exploring new methods for nonviolent conflict resolution).

- Stress that the partnership society is not a leaderless, laissez-faire, or unstructured society. As many of the experiences of people in the 1960s show, such an approach does not work. There are leaders in both a dominator and a partnership society. But since power is defined very differently, so is leadership.

- In the dominator model, power is defined as "power over" and leadership is equated with control. In the partnership model, power is viewed primarily as "power to" or "power with" (actualizing rather than dominating power). And leadership is equated with the ability to bring forth from others their highest creativity and effectiveness in furthering mutually agreed upon goals.

- It is interesting that this partnership view of leadership is gaining currency in many corporations today, because it leads to higher productivity along with greater job satisfaction. It is also interesting, though rarely noted, that this enabling and more empathic style of leadership often comes very easily to women, as women's socialization has stereotypically stressed the enabling or nurturing of others along with empathy for them. Similarly, in the corporate sector, cooperative teamwork where workers participate in decision making is gaining recognition as a more productive as well as a more enjoyable way of functioning.

- Finally, a partnership society is not to be confused with a utopian or unattainably "ideal" society. Rather, it is a viable alternative to the dominator model — one that guided our social development in the mainstream of our original cultural evolution, and one that is today reemerging more powerfully than ever before in recorded history. Most important, it is a model that requires all of our active cocreation, our commitment to making the personal and social changes that can make it a reality.

Discussion Topics

1. The conventional view is grounded in concepts of capitalism vs. communism, extreme right vs. extreme left, developed countries vs. developing countries, religion vs. secularism, East vs. West, etc. This has produced a high degree of fragmentation and confusion. From the perspective of the contrast between the dominator and partnership models, we can see that the underlying struggle is between these two different possibilities for our society. Using the six major elements of each model (see "Six Contrasts"), reexamine these conventional polarities.

The following are some possible questions:

- What are the similarities between Khomeini's Iran, P. W. Botha's South Africa, and the vision of the United States proposed by men such as Jerry Falwell?

- What are the differences?

- What do abolitionism, pacifism, anarchism, anticolonialism, and environmentalism have in common?

- What does feminism have in common with these movements? In what regard does it differ?

- What does Chapter 11 of *The Chalice and the Blade* suggest to you about the theoretical and practical pros and cons of capitalism? Of socialism? Of communism?

- How do you think "progressive" ideas such as progress, equality, and freedom might have been received by the Kurgan invaders? How would the "Fathers" of the orthodox Church who allied themselves with the Emperor Constantine have received these ideas?

- What do you think are the major similarities and differences between the Kurgans and the Nazis?

- Do punk rock and religious fundamentalism have anything in common? Do these trends represent ways of trying to escape the challenge of transformation?

- What do you think are the implications of the idea that the "modern gylanic thrust may be seen as an adaptive process impelled by the survival impulse of our species"?

2. The international human rights movement was an outgrowth of the eighteenth-century "rights of man" philosophies of thinkers like Locke and Rousseau. In that same century, Mary Wollstonecraft and other thinkers brought up the issue of the rights of women. By the nineteenth century, feminist philosophy was an important cultural strain — but one still generally relegated to the intellectual ghetto of the "woman question." This splitting off or peripheralizing of the question of the rights of one half of humanity (actually the numerical majority) from the mainstream of progressive thought has undermined social and cultural progress, so that almost every step forward has been followed by a regressive step back. Discuss ways to heal this fundamental internal inconsistency in progressive thought and action. Some possible focusing questions:

- How do dominator thought and action (on the right or on the left) integrate the so-called public and private spheres?

- How does the family serve as a microcosm of and training ground for social, political, and economic relations?

- Why was defeating the Equal Rights Amendment to the U.S. Constitution a top agenda item for the American right while its passage was only a secondary or "women's issue" for the liberals and the left?

- How is women's contemporary struggle for reproductive freedom related to human rights? To social and cultural progress? To human survival?

- What can we do to support women in the Third World struggling against laws that still sanction wife beating and genital mutilation?

- What can we do about all laws that rigidly define and impose a secondary social status on women?

- How can we together construct and disseminate an integrated new progressive partnership ideology?

3. What does psychologist David Winter's study of Don Juan (discussed in Chapter 10 of *The Chalice and the Blade*) tell us about the modern fascination with James Bond-type movies and sex/killing films such as *Psycho* and *Snuff*? How do books such

as Kate Millett's *Sexual Politics* further illuminate this problem? How do stories, movies, and scientific studies of equal partnership between women and men strengthen the movement toward a more peaceful and creative world based primarily on affiliation rather than violent confrontation and domination?

4. Discuss how the structure of the workplace is affected by the dominator and partnership models respectively.

- How do you think the first factories might have been designed if a partnership rather than a dominator model of society had been in place during the Industrial Revolution?

- Would sweatshops and assembly lines, where workers became cogs in a machine, have been built?

- How do you think the contemporary partnership trends in the workplace, such as parental leave, attention to day care for children, job sharing, flex time, and other social inventions that stem from an integrated female/male workplace/home partnership approach relate to other social trends?

- How can they be supported and accelerated?

5. Discuss how racism and other forms of scapegoating are built into the mental maps for human relations characteristic of the dominator model.

- How does dominator childrearing lead to scapegoating of "weak" and/or "dangerous" out-groups?

- How does the division of humanity into an in-group of "mankind" and a female "other" predispose us to see differences in terms of superior/inferior rankings?

- How are biases based on race, religion, gender, class, sexual orientation, and ethnicity related and mutually reinforcing?

- How are expressions and jokes that call people "retard" or "spas" remnants from a time when the dominator model was more firmly in place and people with disabilities were treated with cruelty?

- Why do you think psychologists have found that people with antisemitic or racist biases characteristically come from authoritarian families where women and men are assigned rigidly stereotypical gender roles?

- What are the implications for ending racism of the shift from a dominator to a partnership model?

6. The current struggle over comparable worth is basically a struggle over what kind of work should be socially (and thus also monetarily) rewarded.

- What is the intrinsic difference between plumbing repair (which is highly paid) and child care (which is one of the lowest paid professions)? Which one has more social value?

- How do you think our economic models can be modified so that activities conventionally considered "women's work" can be properly valued and rewarded in terms of status and pay?

Supplementary Readings

For full titles and citations, see the References at the end of this book.

T. W. Adorno, Else Frenkel-Brunswick, Daniel Levinson, and R. Nevitt Stanford, *The Authoritarian Personality*

Riane Eisler, *Sacred Pleasure*

Riane Eisler, *Tomorrow's Children*

Riane Eisler, Foundation for the Future: Four Cornerstones

Riane Eisler, "Toward a Partnership Society"

Riane Eisler, Changing the Rules of the Game: Work, Values, and the Future

Riane Eisler and David Loye, "The 'Failure' of Liberalism"

Ronald Fletcher, "The Making of the Modern Family"

Erich Fromm, *Escape from Freedom*

Robert Heilbroner, *The Worldly Philosophers*

bell hooks, *Feminist Theory: From Margin to Center*

Fran Hosken, ed., *Women's International Network News*

Sonia Johnson, *From Housewife to Heretic*

David Loye, *The Healing of a Nation*

Karl Marx and Friedrich Engels, *The Communist Manifesto*

Kate Millett, *Sexual Politics*

Robin Morgan, ed., *Sisterhood Is Global*

Isolina Ricci, *Mom's House, Dad's House*

Miriam Schneir, ed., *Feminism: The Essential Historical Writings*

Dale Spender, *Feminist Theorists*

Gloria Steinem, *Outrageous Acts and Everyday Rebellions*

Cornel West, *Race Matters*

Women's International Network News

Preparation for the Next Session

Remind group members of the readings for the next session. Ask them to make lists of all the books they own or they can think of that support the androcratic system. Do the same for the gylanic system. Bring these lists to the next meeting for discussion.

Closing

As appropriate.

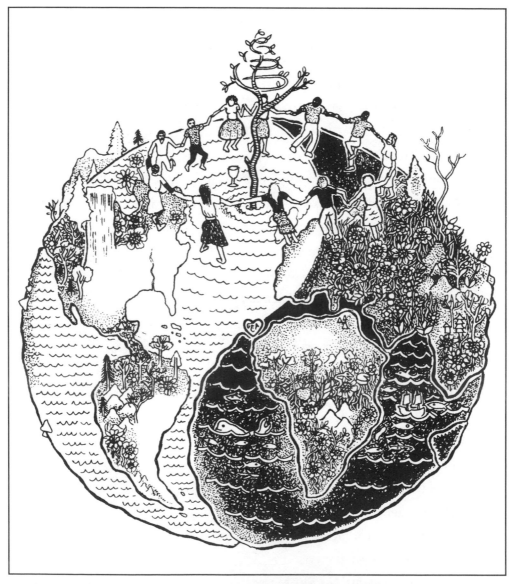

A VISION OF THE "PARTNERSHIP WORLD" BY WRITER, TEACHER, ARTIST, AND ENVIRONMENTAL ACTIVIST JOHN THOMPSON. HERE THOMPSON TURNS A PLAYFUL AND HOPEFUL EYE TOWARD OUR FUTURE.

Session 9
The Evolutionary Crossroads

Goals

1. To consolidate our understanding of the relationship between personal problems and social pathologies.

2. To explore how the global threats of totalitarianism, overpopulation, environmental pollution, and nuclear holocaust relate to stereotypical roles of women and men.

3. To review the cultural transformation theory introduced in *The Chalice and the Blade*.

4. To share our hopes and plans for a partnership future.

5. To explore the possibility of individual and/or group partnership action projects.

Readings

The Chalice and the Blade:
    Chapter 12, "The Breakdown of Evolution: A Dominator Future"
    Chapter 13, "Breakthrough in Evolution: Toward a Partnership Future"
    Review pp. xv-xxiii (from the introduction); pp. 104-106 (on linking and ranking as well as the difference between actualization and domination hierarchies); and pp. 35-137 and pp. 147-155 (on cultural transformation theory)
The Partnership Way:
    Review all Dominator and Partnership charts and text.
    Examine listings of articles in the section called Partnership Resources below and select articles appropriate for chosen action projects.

Materials

Regular supplies.

Preparation for Facilitators

Same as for Session 2.

Getting Started

After the customary opening, the cofacilitators may want to ask each of the participants to share briefly with the group what they think is the most important thing they have gained from the meetings. This is summarized on newsprint by the cofacilitators.

Another way to begin this future-oriented discussion might be to go around the room and ask the participants to share briefly with the group the feelings evoked for them by the closing passage from *The Chalice and the Blade* and, equally important, actions that they think can help translate it into reality.

Closing Passage from *The Chalice and the Blade*

"For above all, this gylanic world will be a world where the minds of children — both girls and boys — will no longer be fettered. It will be a world where limitation and fear will no longer be systematically taught us through myths about how inevitably evil and perverse we humans are. In this world, children will not be taught epics about men who are honored for being violent or fairy tales about children who are lost in frightful woods where women are malevolent witches. They will be taught new myths, epics, and stories in which human beings are good; men are peaceful; and the power of creativity and love — symbolized by the sacred Chalice, the holy vessel of life — is the governing principle. For in this gylanic world, our drive for justice, equality, and freedom, our thirst for knowledge and spiritual illumination, and our yearning for love and beauty will at last be freed. And after the bloody detour of androcratic history, both women and men will at last find out what being human can mean."

After some discussion, facilitators should bring the group focus to the question of how the participants think they can best apply what they have gained from these sessions to their own lives. This is a continuation of the work of the last session, using the charts as working models. But it takes the process one step further — to an exploration of individual and/or group partnership action projects.

Developing Partnership Action Projects

Some of the group members will want to continue to meet. Others may not find this possible or may not be interested. But people in groups who have shared important experiences often want to remain in touch. Specific partnership action projects can now provide the logical next step. As a result of these weeks of joint exploration, members of the group now have the information base for personal and social transformation. Now is the time to try out this new knowledge with a specific action project.

To prompt discussion, you may want to ask:

- What are the best opportunities for partnership social action that lie close at hand in our lives? In our own community?

- What are some specific actions that can help heal the wounds we all carry from dominator child raising and other dominator social interactions?

- How can we most effectively demonstrate in our own lives that the personal *is* political?

To develop a partnership action project, through discussion decide on a specific area to focus on. For example, the human rights article at the Partnership Supplement on the Web suggests that laws can be important vehicles for accelerating partnership change. The technology article (also on the Web) stresses the essential role of the media of communication. This entails not just recognizing how dominator myths have held us back, but most urgently, the creation of alternative stories and images of partnership.

Here are some specific ideas.

Media Action

Social observers increasingly recognize that much of what we see in films and on TV reinforces destructive attitudes and behaviors. The barrage of "fun" violence, mechanical, conquest-oriented sex, and the consumerization of all aspects of a human interaction, serve to deny the reality both of human suffering and of joy. Perhaps most insidious is how this deadening of our emotions through one rapid fragmentized image after another deadens our sense of empathy, even for ourselves.

The sheer mass and frequency of negative images — of "fun" violence, of bad news, of sitcoms based on "hilarious" insensitivity and manipulativeness — also serves another key dominator purpose. It keeps us trapped in an escapist mode.

Even when mass media programs are not blatant dominator propaganda (as in the idealization of a James Bond or Rambo male and the presentation of women as the violent hero's prizes), they communicate a basic sense of powerlessness, indeed of hopelessness: a message that everything is trivial and that there is nothing to do about it except vicariously to "enjoy" an essentially meaningless ride until we die.

If we are to change our mass media, and our lives, for the better, we need to act. As George Gerbner (1993), Dean Emeritus of the Annenberg School for Communication and Professor of Telecommunications at Temple University, writes, a child today is born into a home in which television is on an average of seven hours a day. American adults spend one-third of their freely disposable time with television — more than the next ten highest ranked leisure time activities put together. In short, television has become a major factor in how we as a nation view ourselves and the world.

As Gerbner also notes (1995), the violence-laden media cultivates an exaggerated sense of insecurity and mistrust, a gnawing anxiety about the mean world represented on television. Media violence is an integral part of an increasingly conglomerated and centralized media production and distribution system that has drifted out of demo-cratic reach, creating the cultural envionment in which we all live. The work of Gerbner and other media analysts shows that this "mean world syndrome" has been a major factor in the drift of the political center to the right in the last few decades. Media violence is also increasingly recognized as an important factor in the growing violence of children against both other children and adults.

The average child is likely to have watched 8,000 screen murders and more than 100,000 acts of violence by the end of elementary school — a figure that will again double by the end of his or her teen years (Berry 1993). In children's cartoons there are on average 25 violent incidents per hour (Berry 1993). On top of this, there are hardly ever any consequences to the mayhem. In fact, violence is presented as happy, funny, and of course, manly.

In addition to the pervasive representation of violence in both television enter-tainment and news, another major problem is the underrepresentation and misrepre-sentation of women, minorities, the elderly, the poor, and the disabled in the mass media. The extensive and painstaking studies of the Cultural Indicators Project at the Annenberg School for Communication, University of Pennsylvania, showed that the television conception of Americans is incredibly biased and distorted.

The ratio of boys and men to women and girls, for example, is two to one on television — that is, children and adults see twice as many males as females. This is a subliminal way of communicating the message that males are more important than females — echoing and reinforcing other such cultural messages; for example, the fact that most of what has traditionally been taught as important knowledge in our schools and universities is by and about men.

On programs for children — whose minds are even more easily influenced — this message is even more blatant. Women play only one out of every four roles in children's programs and mature women rarely appear in these shows — and when they do it is primarily as the "evil witch" (Gerbner 1995).

Women are only one out of every five of those who make news on TV. They age faster than men, and as they age they are portrayed as evil and unsuccessful. In fact, women and minorities are disproportionately cast as victims and in roles where they fail, giving the false impression that they are not only less important than white males but also less competent.

It is up to us to change these biased and damaging portrayals of our world, not through censorship, but through concerted and sensible action. To these ends, Gerbner, in conjunction with representatives of many grassroots organizations (including the Center for Partnership Studies) founded the Cultural Environment Movement (CEM). The Cultural Environment Movement is dedicated to working for freedom, fairness, gender equity, general diversity, and democratic decision-making in mass media ownership, employment, and representation.

If you form a media action group, you can affiliate yourselves with CEM by contacting them at 3508 Market Street, Suite B-030, Philadelphia, Pennsylvania 19104; telephone: 215-204-6434; fax: 215-204-5823; email: cem@libertynet.org. You could call yourselves the Partnership Media Action Group and print stationary and use it to make your voices heard.

For example, you can look for good articles and shows that express partnership values. They do appear — all the time! Collaborate in writing letters of praise to the writers, producers, network, local newspaper, sponsors — whoever and whatever will encourage more of this. Creative media people who stick out their necks to do good things need your support — and groups can have much greater impact than individuals.

Groups can also enlist other groups, from the PTA to women's groups such as the YWCA and American Association of University Women, to join in working on the "One for One: It's Only Fair" CEM initiative. This project focuses on the underrepresentation and misrepresentation of women, minorities, the elderly, the disabled, and the poor in the mass media. Its starting point is the jarring fact noted above: that in television casting men outnumber women by a ratio of two to one. Hence the name""One for One" — as a first goal towards accuracy and fairness in media representation.

Because women make up slightly more than 50% of the population, there should be equal representation of women and men on television. For every major male role there should be a major female role — and women should be cast in as many successful and leadership roles as men. This is not only a matter of fair and responsible programming; it is also an important way of cutting down on the violence in television. Because women have stereotypically been associated with nonviolent and caring behaviors, after the first spate of females in violent roles this should also increase the number of positive role models of nonviolent and caring behaviors.

Girls' organizations such as the Girls Scouts should be invited to join in this project, as should elementary and secondary school teachers who can ask children to report back on the frequency and nature of female roles on TV. Magazines such as TV Guide could be approached to run results of these surveys, along with letters from children, teachers, and parents sensitized to the importance of this issue for children and adults alike.

Art Action

Art can expand our consciousness. It can evoke strong emotions, particularly emotions of empathy, outrage, or delight. But the same dominator messages that pervade much of the media also provide the underlying message of much of what has been called great art: from the Greek friezes idealizing killing to the many "great" paintings idealizing rape; for example, Rubens' famous *Rape of the Sabine Women*. Much of modern art, like the mass media it often parodies, communicates a message of hopelessness and meaninglessness.

The currently fashionable deconstructionism certainly highlights the shallowness of much of contemporary pop culture. But while its intent may be one of social criticism, it seems to assume that the only role for the artist is that of disenchanted, indeed disgusted, observer and that the only function of art is as a social mirror, a reflection of alienating, fragmenting, and often horrifying but essentially empty reality.

Such assumptions serve to maintain the dominator system. Fortunately, there are more and more artists who understand that the deconstruction of conventional images is only the first step, that is merely a door to the next step: the reconstruction of "reality" through new/old mythic images and stories. As artist and writer Suzie Gablik notes, the partnership art movement is "reconstructionism" — as reconstructive artists embrace the challenge and responsibility of being orchestrators of culture and consciousness. In her book, *The Reenchantment of Art*, Gablik writes that art has a key role to play in accelerating the transformation from a dominator culture to a partnership culture in all aspects of our lives.

Groups choosing art action could bring together several local artists whose work they think expresses partnership. Get them to read *The Chalice and the Blade, Sacred Pleasure* — or any good summary — and then work with them to define for yourselves what partnership art is. Next, identify more local "partnership" artists using these criteria. Then work with a good local art gallery to stage your own pioneering partnership art exhibit.

The last chapter of *Sacred Pleasure* and the section on art in Chapter Seven of *Tomorrow's Children* are good resources here.

Education Action

Education is a prime vehicle for cultural transformation that each of us can, and must, use. Riane Eisler's book, *Tomorrow's Children: Education for the 21st Century* provides guidelines for developing an integrated partnership curriculum for kindergarten through twelfth grade. It also offers a wealth of resources that can immediately be used in existing schools as well as for self-directed learning through homeschooling for subjects ranging from mathematics and the life sciences to literature, history, and current events.

Tomorrow's Children offers alternative narratives that emphasize human possibilities rather than limitations. It is gender-balanced and pluralistic, with a strong environmental emphasis. It is a tool for teaching sound values. It helps us learn the skills needed to better understand the dominator and partnership aspects of our culture. Most important it provides the educational foundations for building a more equitable and sustainable personal and social future.

Another resource for education is the companion book to *Tomorrow's Children* called *Learning for Living: Fifteen Partnership Literacies and Competencies.*

Using these resources, groups that choose education action can organize Partnership Education Task Forces. A first step is to hold meetings to introduce partnership curriculum materials to teachers, administrators, parents, and students. These meetings can lead to a variety of results ranging from incorporating partnership curriculum materials in existing curricula to their incorporation in teacher education courses in universities and in continuing teacher education programs.

The development of lesson plans for specific applications is an exciting task. There are some of these materials in *Tomorrow's Children*, but many more are needed. The Center for Partnership Studies (CPS) is planning to establish a Clearinghouse for Partnership Education. We ask that you send lesson plans developed through your action groups to us so we may make them available to others through this clearinghouse. (See page 205 for information about CPS).

An even more ambitious goal is the formation of a number of pilot partnership schools. This will require funding and a great deal of energy and active participation by dedicated women and men. Perhaps your group can pioneer this much needed, exciting venture!

The need for partnership material is urgent, and every one of us can contribute.

If you have a knack for drawing, you might also try your hand at children's picture books, posters, or cartoons. Whatever the area, work with sympathetic teachers with experience in curricula in your area of interest. When you've got a product that looks good, give it exposure through talks to open-minded PTAs, school superintendents, and school board members. And again, please be sure to send us a copy for the Clearinghouse.

Economic Action

A major engine for cultural transformation is economic action. We urgently need a new partnership economics that integrates the best aspects of both capitalism and socialism, but goes further to recognize the economic value of the most foundationally productive work: the work of caring and caretaking.

Today the work of caring and caretaking is more urgently needed than ever before. As we see all around us, environmental caretaking may be a survival requisite. The work of caring for children, the elderly, and the sick in families has always been a survival requisite, but since in the dominator model it is considered "women's work" to be done for free in a male controlled household, it has not even been included in calculations of economic productivity such as GDP (Gross Domestic Product) and GNP (Gross National Product) unless it is monetized. And even then, as in childcare, it is accorded very low economic value. Childcare workers (a primarily female occupation) are paid substantially less than plumbers (a primarily male occupation) — despite the obvious fact that caring for children is not only more socially important, but requires more skill and knowledge.

This reflects what Riane Eisler, in *The Chalice and the Blade* and other works, calls the alienation of caring labor. This is the systematic unconscious according of lower, or no, value to work stereotypically considered feminine in dominator societies.

The Center for Partnership Studies, in partnership with the Global Futures Foundation and other organizations, is establishing a Clearinghouse for Economic Inventions that Recognize the Value of Caring and Caretaking. Economic action groups can play an important part in this exciting venture.

You can collect information on economic inventions such as parental leave and on-site childcare (including provisions for nursing stations) and show how they work for both business and employees (reducing absenteeism, increasing productivity, and, most important, providing good nurturing). You can write up this kind of information, publicize it through your community, talk to your employers and government officials about it — and send us your findings and the results of your efforts in concise form for the Clearinghouse.

A good resource here is Riane Eisler's article "Changing the Rules of the Game: Work, Values, and Our Future," which, like other articles listed in the Partnership Resources can be downloaded from the Holistic Education Press website or ordered from them by readers of this book. This article describes movement towards partnership economic inventions that recognize the value of caring and caretaking.

You can hold focus groups and other meetings, bringing together people from all walks of life to brainstorm new partnership economic inventions. In these meetings, highlight how the redesign of the workplace and the movement towards a partnership family go hand in hand. For example, since unfortunately, we still have a gendered double standard of value in which what men do is more highly valued, if men share with women the caring for children and the housekeeping, this in turn will accelerate the higher valuing of this socially essential work.

These groups can also discuss and educate others about the negative social-economic consequences for us all of this devaluation of caring and caretaking work.

For example, politicians in recent years have found it increasingly difficult to justify budgets that allocate significant sums to "welfare" services — or caring for others — as many of their constituents do not think that caring for people's welfare is economically valuable. Similarly, since women are stereotypically associated with cleaning up the family's living quarters, corporations have not given high value (or sufficient funding) to manufacturing processes that do not produce industrial waste that today increasingly clutter up our national and global living quarters.

Partnership economic action projects can design and present programs to educate people about these issues. This would also raise awareness about a point stressed in both the human rights article and Chapters 11 and 13 of *The Chalice and the Blade*: there is a need for moving from the male as norm (whether in the design of cars, factories, or religious and political institutions) to a new gender-holistic or partnership model. In other words, it means leaving behind the stereotypes and paying attention to the real needs of both girls and boys, women and men, for a family and work environment that supports and enhances everyone's well-being, productivity, and creativity.

Environmental Action

The mix of the dominator model and high technology is at the root of our growing environmental crisis. Certainly action is essential to raise consciousness about rain forests (the lungs of our planet), the health risk of pollution and holes in the ozone layer, saving dolphins, and resource depletion through wasteful overconsumption. But as long as the notion of humans' right (and need) to dominate and conquer nature prevails, we are like the legendary boy putting his finger in the hole in the dike. What is needed is a fundamental shift in consciousness about the connectedness or linking of all life forms on this planet and our responsibility in our cultural and technological evolution to act in harmony with nature, rather than just to exploit it. Here partnership education — including knowledge of the old mythology about the Earth as our mother — comes in.

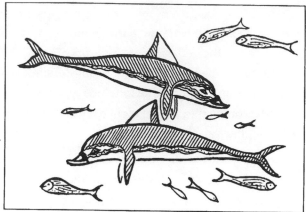

MODERN ECOLOGY
POSTER? WHAT WE
THINK OF AS
ECOLOGICAL
CONSEQUENCES IS
VISIBLE IN THIS
3500-YEAR-OLD
FRESCO FROM CRETE.
LINE DRAWING BY
JIM BEEMAN FROM
THE ORIGINAL.

A specific example of how this new/old story can be communicated relates to the dolphin and the ancient Minoans, who lived in more harmonious partnership with one another and with nature. They felt so connected with the dolphin that it is frequently portrayed in their art. A vivid example, which could be reproduced for a Partnership Ecology education project, is the beautiful dolphin fresco in the Palace at Knossos — which looks remarkably like a three-thousand-year-old precursor of a modern ecology poster. Showing how what we call our ecological consciousness is rooted in ancient traditions can greatly accelerate its acceptance. Just as important is showing that an environmental consciousness cannot just be tacked on to a dominator model. A sustainable future requires the transformation of basic values and institutions. The higher valuing of the environment found in Minoan society as exemplified in an art that celebrates all aspects of nature was not isolated. It was part of a culture that oriented primarily to the partnership model — one in which women and the stereotypically feminine were also highly valued.

In more affluent nations such as the United States, which consumes a disproportionate percentage of the world's resources, overconsumption and wastefulness are major ecological issues, as they contribute to both natural resources depletion and such environmental health hazards as our mountains of toxic waste. Once again, this problem is rooted in a dominator model of relations.

One of the reasons people overconsume is that this serves as a substitute for the self-esteem and satisfying interpersonal relationships that are so difficult to build in a dominator-oriented society. Therefore another basic element in ecology education is to help people see these connections more clearly. This could help to counterbalance the false promises of ads that literally create addictions to unnecessary and often even harmful purchasing and overconsumption. An important byproduct of such a partnership education project would be the freeing of time, energy, and money to focus, not on more material accumulations, but on the only accumulations that are truly lasting: our human relations and our human development, both individually and socially.

Good resources here are the materials on the environment in *Sacred Pleasure*, the chart from *Sacred Pleasure* at the end of this book, as well as *Tomorrow's Children* and *Learning for Living*.

Personal Action and Community Building

Remember, a group begins with two. You might choose a personal project, such as the creation of a partnership relationship with someone you live with. Keep a progress journal to review together. Or together carry out research, like making a list of partnership literature, movies, or TV programs, and disseminate it through schools, churches, and other organizations. (A good resource is *Tomorrow's Children*.)

Again, we are here dealing with action linked to fundamental changes in consciousness. In psychological terms, it means moving from a defense-needs to a growth-needs motivational system where fear (and hence the "need" to control) is not obstacles to partnership between women and men, women and women, men and men, children and children, children and parents — and between nations and nations. It also means taking an even closer look at the prison of the "macho" role, which goes along with the manipulative and subtly controlling and devious female stereotype of the "Total Woman," both of which keep us locked in the "war of the sexes" and its corollaries, warfare and the conquest of nature.

Another personal action project would be to have the members of this group commit to form an ongoing personal and family support system. This is not a new partnership idea, as it has been an important component in many social movements, from Quakers to women's support groups. It is a very effective and practical way of providing concrete personal and family support, such as helping to care for one another's children and bringing food and medicine if someone is sick. It is also a very effective means of partnership community building. These local partnership communities could eventually come together and form national and international communities of mutual encouragement and support. Such links with like-minded and like-hearted individuals and families are wonderful as a way of enriching our lives and feeling more comfortable and secure, for example, if one is traveling. Most important, they can be the basis for concerted and lasting social action and positive change.

For other ideas, see "Partnership Action: A Quick Guide" in Additional Exercises and Topics for Discussion.

Political Action

A point emphasized in *The Chalice and the Blade*, *Sacred Pleasure*, *Tomorrow's Children*, and *Learning for Living* is that the personal is political. What we do in our personal lives is inextricably connected with the larger, so-called public sphere of politics and economics. This is a two-way dynamic. Changes in our personal lives lead to social changes. But to effectively improve our personal lives — to heal ourselves — we have to heal society. In other words, without fundamental changes in belief systems, laws, policies, and institutions our personal healing can go only so far and no further.

Perhaps nowhere is this as apparent as in the effect of public policies and laws on economic and social development in the so-called developing world: the nations with the greatest poverty and hunger. There are tremendous economic, social, and cultural obstacles to improving the quality of life — indeed, all too often to saving lives — in the developing world rooted in dominator values and institutions. By the same token, on our planet — so shrunken by incredibly powerful technologies of communication and transportation, as well as destruction — what happens in the developing world will also profoundly effect our own chances for personal growth, and even survival. Hence, we need to think of partnership political action globally, supporting the partnership movement worldwide.

In Chapter 12 of *The Chalice and the Blade*, the relationship between war and peace, ecological balance or imbalance, and so-called women's issues is discussed. The point is made that the kinds of policies required to maintain a dominator/androcratic system are on a potentially lethal collision course with the policies that can lead to a sustainable and vastly improved future.

The most urgent case in point is the policies required to deal with the global population explosion that poses a massive threat not only to the quality of all of our lives but to our very survival as a species on our planet.

Among the Online Partnership Resources you will find "Women, Development, and the Population: Highlights from the 1989 State of World Population Report" by Dr. Nafis Sadik, executive director of the United Nations Population Fund, which more than any previous United Nations document on the subject clearly shows the essential link between raising the status of Third World women and economic and social development for all. This important document makes specific recommendations that could be the inspiration and basis for political action projects.

Another good source of ideas for political action is Chapter 18 of *Sacred Pleasure*, "Toward a New Politics of Partnership." It shows that we are on the threshold of a new integrated politics of partnership: one where particular attention is given to challenging entrenched traditions of domination and violence in the so-called private sphere of parent-child as well as sexual and other intimate relations.

The article by Riane Eisler called "Foundations for the Future: Four Corner-stones" available online proposes an international campaign against violence and abuse in early childhood as well as an international campaign for gender equity and nonviolence. Political action groups may want to work on local aspects of these two foundational ventures. You may want to involve your church, synagogue, PTA, professional organization, or other groups in these exciting and essential political strategies for laying the foundations for a more peaceful and more equitable world. You could hold discussion sessions and organize conferences. You could support existing organizations working toward these ends.

The main thing is to raise consciousness, shift the focus of public discourse to foundational issues, and encourage and participate in action. For example, you may want to talk to your priest or minister and urge him or her to preach against the sins of sexual violence rather than sexual pleasure. You may want to encourage them to make the themes of domination and partnership in all relations — both those conventionally considered personal and political — a key theme. You could discuss the problems with groups such as the Promise Keepers, who offer men the false choice of being irresponsible to their families or taking control of their families — emphasizing the partnership alternatives.

Political action groups may want to also look at the section on economic action and pursue some of the projects listed there. Indeed, all of these action groups are interconnected. What we need is systemic change. But economics and politics have tended to be ignored in much of the personal growth and healing movement. Hence the importance of these action groups.

There are many excellent existing grassroots organizations and projects world-wide, some of which are listed in the last two chapters of *Sacred Pleasure*. For example, S.E.W.A. in India, The Grameen Bank Project of Bangladesh, the Katalysis and the Earth Trust Foundation, and Women's World Banking administer village loans to women for various productive products and enterprises. Women's World Banking and the Global Fund for Women make larger loans and grants. These are empowering to women, both economically and politically, and represent important steps toward real democracy worldwide. Some groups may want to link with these organizations and support them. Others may want to concentrate efforts on educating policy makers, since U.S. aid projects can be exponentially more effective once they recognize the centrality of women to economic, social, and political progress.

Some people have been under the illusion that they can be apolitical by not getting involved, not voting. But, in fact, these are political acts. By sitting apathetically by and doing nothing, we allow others to have much more political power, giving much more weight to their votes and actions. The notion that if a politician compromises we should not vote for her or him is equally misguided. The fact is that there must be compromise in politics. Even if it is voting for what we may consider "the lesser of two evils," it is essential to vote. Indeed, it is irresponsible not to vote. This is evidenced by the tremendous suffering caused in recent years when a highly organized, disciplined, and well-funded minority elected a new U.S. Congress that enacted regressive policies. One goal of partnership political action groups is to communicate the importance of participation in the American democratic process. Another is to strengthen this process by helping people understand the importance of voting for representatives who will back real campaign finance reform.

If the group — or part of it — wants to launch its own partnership action project, discussion and planning will likely take up most of the remaining time for this closing session.

However, all or part of the group may want to continue discussions, either based on *The Chalice and the Blade* or continuing with *Sacred Pleasure* and from there going on to *Tomorrow's Children* and *Learning for Living*. For groups who want to continue with *Sacred Pleasure*, the section called "The Partnership Way for *Sacred Pleasure*" on page 117 below will be useful.

Topics for Continuing Discussion

1. We know that by reexamining our personal and family history we can begin to change unhealthy habits of functioning. We are now also learning that many painful habits are the result of having had to function in a dominator system.

- What are the implications of a dominator system for our self-image and self-esteem as women and men?

- How does the sense of failure experienced by many men relate to the stereotypical expectations of the male role as being on of one-upmanship: of sexual "scoring," of "winning" or "losing" in the workplace, of always being in control?

- How do women's well-known problems with self-esteem relate to the still-prevalent myths about female sinfulness, inferiority, and untrustworthiness?

- What are the implications of the dominator model for sexual relations? For example, how do incest, sexual harassment, and rape relate to the dominator stereotype of a masculinity associated with domination and violence? Do children's cartoons where the hero kills the villain and then gets the girl subliminally associate sex with violence? Do plays like *Othello* implicitly justify the killing of sexually independent women? What is the message to girls about their bodies from Barbie dolls, who if a real woman with her proportions would fracture her spine? What is the message of women's fashion magazines? What messages do publications such as *Hustler*, with its many images linking sexual arousal and brutality, send to boys and men? Reading *Sacred Pleasure* will stimulate this discussion.

- What are the implications of the dominator systems for our family relations? For example, how does what we today call codependency or addiction to abusive and unhealthy relationships (where an individual seeks to manipulate or placate an abusive family member) relate to the stereotypical passive feminine role in a dominator family? How do men's familiar problems with forming intimate relations relate to the stereotypical image of the "strong" or "macho" man as not needing anyone else?

- What are the implications of the dominator system for race relations? For example, how are the myths of the "happy nigger" and the "contented housewife" related? How are racial segregations and the rigid segregation of women in fundamentalist Muslim regimes such as post-Khomeini's Iran and the Taliban of Afghanistan related?

2. One of the major themes of Chapter 12 of *The Chalice and the Blade* and of Chapter 18 of *Sacred Pleasure* is the impossibility of implementing the kinds of policies that can effectively counter the global threats of totalitarianism, overpopulation, environmental pollution, and nuclear holocaust while attempting to maintain a dominator system founded on the stereotypical male/female roles. How do you think both the general public and policymakers can quickly be made aware of this critical issue? The following questions may be helpful in exploring this area.

- How do you think world hunger, malnutrition, desertification, low levels of competency and education, and other pressing problems of development and survival would be affected by an approach to global development in which women's needs and aspirations were central rather than peripheral? (Chapter 12 of *The Chalice and the Blade*; Chapter 17 of *Sacred Pleasure*; *Women, Men, and the Global Quality of Life*; *Women in Poverty*, edited by Devaki Jain and Nirmala Bannerjee; and the human rights article by Riane Eisler listed in the Partnership Resources section may be particulary relevant here.)

- Why do so many people (including scientists and other experts) express such grave concerns about the population explosion, mounting ecological disasters, the threat of economic collapse, etc., while others predict only minimal problems that will by and large take care of themselves?

- How do you think this relates to the mixed dominator and partnership messages received from politicians and the media?

- How do you feel about the United States' official abandonment during the 1980s and 1990s of a world leadership role in population control, family planning, equal rights for women, ecological protection, and the exploration of solar power and other decentralizing alternatives to nuclear power?

- What is the role of education in either maintaining the dominator elements of our culture or strengthening the partnership elements?

- What knowledge and skills will young people need to both more effectively deal with the problems stemming from the dominator model and to play an active part in the shift to the partnership model? (Excerpt from *Tomorrow's Children* and *Learning for Living* can help stimulate this discussion.)

- What feelings, thoughts, and possible actions are evoked in you by the statement that "a dominator future is sooner or later almost certainly a future of global nuclear war — and the end of all of humanity's problems and aspirations"?

3. Some theoretical issues may bear clarification. For example:

- How does the cultural transformation theory differ from the conventional linear or straight-line states of cultural evolution approach?

- How would you describe the difference between actualization and domination hierarchies?

- How do you see the relationship between "productive" and "destructive" approaches to conflict in terms of Jean Baker Miller's analysis?

- How would you describe alternative views of power in terms of concepts such as win/win and win/lose, or Jean Baker Miller's differentiation of "power for oneself" from "power over others?"

- How would you describe partnership healing? How does it differ from many conventional approaches? Can you think of specific instances of both types and of ways to encourage the growth of partnership healing? (John Robbins' book *Reclaiming Our Health* can stimulate this discussion.)

- What does the phrase "alienation of caring labor" mean to you? (Chapter 17 of *Sacred Pleasure* and the article "Changing the Rules of the Game" listed in the Partnership Resources Section are useful here.)

- How can we use technology to accelerate the shift from domination to partnership?

- How can we use the media?

- How can we use the political process?

- How can we involve the corporate sector?

- How can we work through our churches and other religious institutions?

Supplementary Readings

For full titles and citations, see the References at the end of this book.

Lester R. Brown, *State of the World 1995*

Helen Caldicott, *Nuclear Madness*

Fritjof Capra, *The Turning Point*

Rachel Carson, *Silent Spring*

Riane Eisler, *Sacred Pleasure*

Riane Eisler, *Tomorrow's Children*

Riane Eisler, *Learning for Living*

George Gerbner, "Women and Minorities in Television: A Study in Casting and Fate"

George Gerbner, "Marketing Global Mayhem"

George Gerbner, Larry Gross, Michael Morgan, Nancy Signorielli, "Growing Up with Television: The Cultivation Perspective"

Charlotte Perkins Gilman, *Herland*

Bertram Gross, *Friendly Fascism*

Hazel Henderson, *The Politics of the Solar Age*

Perdita Huston, *Third World Women Speak Out*

Devaki Jain and Nirmala Bannerjee, eds., *Women in Poverty*

Ervin Laszlo, *Evolution*

David Loye, *The Sphinx and the Rainbow*

John McHale, *The Future of the Future*

Jean Baker Miller, *Toward a New Psychology of Women*

Hilkka Pietilä and Jeanne Vickers, *Making Women Matter*

Betty Reardon, *Sexism and the War System*

John Robbins, *Reclaiming Our Health*

Jonas Salk, *Anatomy of Reality*

Gita Sen, *Development, Crises, and Alternative Visions*

Ruth Sivard, *World Military and Social Expenditures*

Charlene Spretnak and Fritjof Capra, *Green Politics*

Robert Theobald, *The Rapids of Change*

Women's International News Network (WIN) News

Closing

The main thing to accomplish in this last session is to leave everyone with a good feeling about themselves, their partners in this new learning experience, and new prospects for a better future.

If the group, or any part of it, is ready to launch a partnership action project, be sure responsibility for this project is in specific hands — newly elected facilitators, or yourselves, if you wish to continue with such a project.

Having gained this valuable experience as partnership discussion group facilitators, however, you may be better off starting another discussion group and encouraging others to spin off action projects — until you're ready to switch roles, for a change. In any case, details such as meeting places and times for spin-off action project, should be decided upon before you part.

If the group, or any part of it, wants to continue discussions using *Sacred Pleasure* (and later perhaps *Tomorrow's Children* and *Learning for Living*) before considering a partnership action project, see that this, too, is properly arranged.

You may want to end this session with some memorable ritual, visualization, or quiet time, but be sure to make it brief. The main thing you want to encourage is the feeling — and expression of this feeling — that over the past few weeks you have participated in a meaningful partnership, and exploration of a new future. Now the task is to work together toward this much better future with hope, with joy, and with a new conviction that it can be ours.

The reconstruction of our belief systems and institutions from a dominator to a partnership culture is in the hands of every one of us. These sessions have provided us with some tools for creative thinking and specific ways of empowering ourselves. Now is the time for action, for personal and social transformation — and it starts with each of us!

A Note to Facilitators

Please send a summary of your group's collective comments and suggestions plus brief summaries of the results of the meetings to us at the Center for Partnership Studies, P. O. Box 51936, Pacific Grove, California 93950.

Additional
Exercises and
Discussion Topics

THIS IS A FIGURE OF THE GODDESS FOUND ON A GOLD PENDANT IN CRETE, DATING
BACK TO 1500 B.C. HER HEADDRESS IS OF PAPYRUS SYMBOLIZING THE LIFE-GIVING
AND SUSTAINING POWERS OF NATURE.
LINE DRAWING BY JOHN MASON FROM THE ORIGINAL.

The Partnership Way for
Sacred Pleasure

Readers of *Sacred Pleasure: Sex, Myths, and the Politics of the Body* are also forming study, discussion, and action groups. *The Partnership Way* is proving a useful resource for these groups. Many of the materials contained in Sessions One through Nine in "The Partnership Study Guide" section of *The Partnership Way* can be used to deepen our understanding of sexuality, spirituality, love, and power.

Sexuality, spirituality, love, and power are the main thematic strands of *Sacred Pleasure*, which probes how we may free our powerful human yearning for caring connection from the fetters of dominator socialization and institutions. Like *The Chalice and the Blade*, *Sacred Pleasure* takes us into our deep prehistoric past. Its focus, however, is on the two main levers of human motivation: pain and pleasure.

Sacred Pleasure shows that much of what we have been taught about ourselves, our bodies, our relationships, as well as about what is possible or impossible, right or wrong, or even sacred or profane, has been distorted. Like *The Chalice and the Blade*, *Sacred Pleasure* traces the massive remything that occurred during the prehistoric shift from societies orienting primarily to the partnership model to societies in which domination and violence became institutionalized, idealized, and even sacralized. But *Sacred Pleasure* probes this shift at an even deeper level. It examines what I call the pleasure to pain shift. It shows that much that is happening in our time is an attempt to reverse this shift so that we may move to a future of partnership sexuality and spirituality, to a society where pleasure, not pain, is the central theme of our sacred and secular imagery — and of our lives.

Part One of *Sacred Pleasure* asks and answers the question "How did we get here?" Part Two asks and answers the question "Where are we and where do we go from here?" Following this sequence, groups using *Sacred Pleasure* as their primary reading material can start with Session One: Getting Acquainted. In this stage-setting session, facilitators in partnership with participants set the goals for the nine meetings.

Facilitators can use the ideas for ceremonies provided in Session One, as well as the exercise called "Visualizing a Partnership World." The questions listed in Session One are equally appropriate for beginning discussions of *Sacred Pleasure*. Participants could also be asked to visualize what images of the sacred would be like in a partnership society. Specifically, would they focus more on pain or on pleasure? What kind of spirituality would be considered normal in such a society? Would it be primarily remote and otherworldly or would it imbue daily acts and our day-to-day relations with the sacred?

Groups would then follow this opening session with Sessions Two through Nine, changing the readings as indicated below. In addition, a tenth session called "New Paths to Power and Love" would be added to accommodate the greater length of *Sacred Pleasure*, and thus the additional readings, as well as to expand the themes of the evolutionary crossroads and action for the future.

Readings

The list of readings from *Sacred Pleasure* that follows can be used as a handout to participants during Session One.

Readings for Session Two: Crisis and Opportunity

Our Sexual and Social Choices: An Introduction

Charts from the back of *The Partnership Way* reprinted from *Sacred Pleasure*

Readings for Session Three: Our Hidden Heritage

Chapter One. From Ritual to Romance: Sexuality, Spirituality, and Society

Chapter Two. Animal Rites and Human Choices: The Roots of Dominator and Partnership Sex

Chapter Three. Sex as Sacrament: The Divine Gifts of Life, Love, and Pleasure

Readings for Session Four: The Essential Difference

Chapter Four. Sex and Civilization: The Early Roots of Western Culture

Readings for Session Five: The Interruption of Civilization

Chapter Five. From Eros to Chaos: Sex and Violence

Chapter Six. The Reign of the Phallus: War, Economics, Morality, and Sex

Readings for Session Six: The Great Cover-Up

Chapter Seven. The Sacred Marriage in a Dominator World: The Metamorphosis of Sex, Death, and Birth

Chapter Eight. The Last Traces of the Sacred Marriage: Mysticism, Masochism, and the Human Need for Love

Readings for Session Seven: The Quest for Peace, Creativity, and Partnership

Chapter Nine. From Ancient to Modern Times: Setting the Stage

Chapter Ten. Waking from the Dominator Trance: The Revolution in Consciousness and the Sexual Revolution

Readings for Session Eight: Breaking Free

Chapter Eleven. Bondage or Bonding: Sex, Spirituality, and Repression

Chapter Twelve. Making Love or Making War: Eroticizing Violence

Chapter Thirteen. Sex, Gender, and Transformation: From Scoring to Caring

Chapter Fourteen. Getting Out of Prince Charming's Slipper: Sex, Femininity, and Power

Readings for Session Nine: The Evolutionary Crossroads

Chapter Fifteen. Sex, Lies, and Stereotypes: Changing Views of Nature, the Body, and Truth

Chapter Sixteen. Morality, Ethics, and Pleasure: Sex and Love in the Age of AIDS

Chapter Seventeen. Sex, Power, and Choice: Redefining Politics and Economics

Readings for Session Ten: New Paths to Power and Love

Chapter Eighteen. Towards a Politics of Partnership: Our Choices for the Future

Chapter Nineteen. The New Eves and the New Adams: The Courage to Question, the Will to Choose, and the Power to Love

Exercises

Facilitators will find that the experiential exercise in Session Three on "Free Association on Women's and Men's Bodies" is tailor-made for *Sacred Pleasure*. In fact, they will find that many of the discussion topics in every session go hand in glove with the salient themes of *Sacred Pleasure*.

For example, on page 74 is the question of why we have religious teachings that human sufferings and injustice are inevitable, even holy, raising the issue of how this perpetuates a dominator society. There is also the question of what the message about human nature is from stories such as those of Adam and Eve and Cain and Abel. Similarly, the discussion questions on page 81, on the parallels between the medieval witch hunts and Muslim fundamentalists torturing, raping, and killing "errant" women today can serve as an entry to themes discussed in depth in *Sacred Pleasure*.

The healing ritual on page 78, particularly the invocation from Starhawk's adaptation of "Charge of the Star Goddess," that "all acts of love and pleasure are my rituals" is also provocative. It leads directly to an exploration of the themes of pain and pleasure addressed in *Sacred Pleasure*.

In addition, facilitators may want to add other exercises. An exercise I have found particularly effective and enjoyable when doing workshops based on *Sacred Pleasure* is a moving meditation that goes as follows:

Participants are first asked to first clasp hands in a circle. Next, they are asked to gently release their partners' hands and drop their arms to their sides. Moving very slowly and breathing deeply, they are asked to begin moving their arms gently in front of their chests, about a centimeter away from their body, palms toward the body. Moving very slowly without interruption, the movement then continues with the arms and hands crossing in front of the face, opening up into what I call the chalice position. In this position, upper arms are held high, parallel to shoulders, with forearms at a right angle vertically, palms facing inward.

Arms stay momentarily uplifted in this chalice position (the position of blessing we see in friezes of ancient priestesses, still used by popes and priests today), palms facing inward, paralleling the ears and head. This position is only held for a few seconds, all the time breathing deeply, feeling the energy flow through the body.

After this minipause, the movement continues with palms still facing inward, moving upward into a dome, like a lid on the chalice, with middle fingers touching, held about a half foot over the crown of the head. This position is held for a few moments to feel the energy flowing down through the head and body, feet firmly grounded on the floor.

Then, again very, very slowly, hands come down and forward, palms facing towards the head, crossing first on top of the head, then moving downward, in front of the face and chest and heart. Hands should not touch. One hand is held in front of the other, thumbs parallel, pointing up, the other fingers forming butterfly wings. Hands should be only centimeters from the face and body, moving very slowly downward.

When hands come to the solar plexus, they pause a moment before continuing down to the groin. Here hands pause another minisecond, before releasing and hanging on the side of the body.

From there the movement begins again, hands moving in front of the body, crossing in front as described above. The same cycle of movement is repeated three times, with the facilitator speaking softly, gently, slowly, reminding participants to breathe and providing directions and demonstrating.

Participants report that they feel grounded and at peace, with a real sense of healing energy flowing through them. In other words, this is a moving meditation, possibly one with very, very ancient roots that we are today recreating.

After this, participants can be asked to share their feelings, as well as how this kind of worship compares to kneeling or prostrating oneself on the floor. Alternately, this exercise can be used as a closing for each session. Or it can be used as an opening, whatever facilitators and the group wish.

Another suggestion is to close each session with a quote chosen by facilitators from various chapters in *Sacred Pleasure*. For example, facilitators may want to use the poem by David Loye on pages 398-399 of *Sacred Pleasure* to introduce Session Six (The Great Cover-Up), even though this takes it out of the order of readings from the book.

They could use the opening paragraphs of Chapter One to introduce Session Two, using the following quote to initiate discussion:

> Candles, music, flowers, and wine — these we all know are the stuff of romance, of sex, and of love. But candles, flowers, music, and wine are also the stuff of religious ritual, of our most sacred rites.

> Why is there this striking, though seldom noted, commonality? Is it just accidental that *passion* is the word we use for both sexual and mystical experiences? Or is there here some long-forgotten but still powerful connection?

Another passage that can be used, perhaps for Session Nine or Ten is from the last chapter of *Sacred Pleasure* "The New Eves and the New Adams," on page 399:

> If we succeed in completing the shift from a dominator to a partnership world, both the realities and myths of our future will be very different than from what they are now. For in this world we will be far more able to fully utilize all our senses and capacities — including senses and capacities we did not even know we had — to create the new institutional forms and myths that will make it possible for us to fully express the miracle, mystery, and joy of what mystics throughout the ages have called the sacred truth of our oneness in love.

The Partnership Way
for Multicultural
Community-Based Education

Christine Sleeter and
Carmen Montecinos

Engaging teachers in community-based learning that is structured around part-nership principles can show them ways in which power can be shared among school professionals and with other school constituencies. The following is a fictionalized composite portrait of a community-based teacher education project that illustrates partnership relationships. It is important to keep in mind that social practices, insti-tutions, and people rarely enact pristine versions of the parntership and dominator models. In practice, organizations based on the partnership model distinguish them-selves from those based on the dominator model more in terms of the degree or emphasis given to things such as cooperation versus competition, trust versus fear, linking versus ranking, and so on.

A Community-Based Learning Project
Based on Partnership Intelligence

Central College's teacher education program has a network of field experiences throughout the program that link the college, community organizations, schools, and progressive community grassroots movements. Like most other teacher education programs in the U.S., the majority of the students are white and many are from suburban or small town communities. Central College has been working hard to recruit future teachers from urban and rural communities of color in the local area through this college-community-school network.

As is true in most low-income communities, a wide variety of community agencies exist, run by a wide variety of people. The network began informally, and although it now has some formal structure, it still rests on an informal basis of mutuality. The college faculty members who developed the community component of the curriculum over time developed collaborative relationships with people in a few community organizations and schools. For example, one faculty member is on the board of the local affiliate of the National Urban League (a predominantly African American social service and civil rights organization), and another is on the board of the local chapter of LULAC (League of United Latin American Citizens, also a civil rights organization). About half of the faculty live in or adjacent to the inner city. Some are members of local Black or Latino churches. As a result, they can orient their thinking regarding the needs of the community largely around the perspectives of the community members. The faculty have identified three goals for their students: to learn about the community from the perspectives of people who live there, to become acquainted with issues faced by the community, and to become acquainted with the political and educational work community people engage in to address these issues. To accomplish these goals, they sought partnerships with community agencies and community centers that were run primarily by community members. The faculty got to know some of the directors and staff members of these agencies, and explored ways in which college student volunteers might be of help to the agencies and centers. For example, the local Urban League and a partner community center had several programs that could use volunteer help; they also needed help developing a newsletter and upgrading computer systems. The faculty were also especially interested in political action and advocacy efforts in the community, wanting teachers to critique and begin to challenge mainstream views that represented inner-city dwellers as the source of their problems in the areas of housing, health, education, safety, and so on. In the case of the Urban League, although its mission was to serve the community rather than to work politically, many of its members were also members of the local chapter of the NAACP, which was very active politically, met regularly at the Urban League facility, and was willing to discuss with the university students their perspectives on the political tasks involved in community development.

At the same time, faculty members were also developing collaborative relationships with local schools. For example, several teachers were interested in improving literacy instruction, and were especially interested in using multicultural children's literature, helping Spanish-speaking students develop biliteracy skills, incorporating traditional family stories into literacy instruction, involving parents, and teaching students to create books about their own communities. The faculty and teachers worked together to develop strategies that fit the students in the schools, involving teacher education students in this process.

As they went through the teacher education program, students experienced field placements in both community centers and schools. From their perspectives, there was remarkable continuity among the schools, the college, and the community, since the people they worked with knew each other and collaborated in a variety of contexts. No one seemed to be "the" expert on issues. The students also experienced a fair amount of dissonance and disagreement; however, they discovered that there was no monolithic "inner city" perspective, but rather great variety in how people identified and viewed issues and situations such as how to approach Black English. By the time they finished student teaching, the teacher education students appreciated the complexity of issues teachers face, and the impossibility of representing cultural groups in monolithic terms, and they respected the diverse perspectives and areas of expertise of adults in the local community.

There was no dichotomy between service provider and recipient; rather, there was a fairly horizontal network of service exchange. The community organizations with which Central College worked were largely indigenous to the local community. Even the Urban League, an affiliate of a national organization, was directed by an African American professional who lived in the community and was staffed by people who also lived in the community. While many of the people involved were not necessarily politically active, they shared the social locations, perspectives, cultures, and languages of the local community. The community organizations themselves worked as partners with local residents. In addition, the college faculty had developed partnership relations with the organizations, and with some local residents and teachers. Most of the teacher education faculty had not grown up in the local area and about two-thirds were white. As such, they made conscious choices to avoid taking on the role of experts. The partnership relationship was manifest in a variety of ways.

First, students' volunteer work in the community was structured around community needs rather than college convenience. Community center directors selected volunteers based on information students supplied about their skills and available time; some students had to change their own schedules and often their time commitments extended beyond the traditional semester time structure. The college students often had to rely on others in the community organization to teach them what to do. For many, this was the first time they were expected to learn from an adult of color outside of the college. College faculty communicated regularly with the organizations to make sure their time investment was worthwhile to them.

Second, the college, community organizations, and schools had developed visible, collaborative decision-making relationships. It was not unusual for teacher education students to see a college professor conferring with a community center director in the director's office, or college faculty and teachers meeting with parents and community center staff to solve a problem or initiate a program. Some of the structure and content of the teacher education program was, in fact, a product of such collaboration.

Third, through this collaborative working relationship, teacher education students learned to teach in ways that connected with the children's cultural resources. For example, rather than learning to view literacy as a resource the "haves" give to the "have nots," they were learning to see language as richly woven into the daily fabric of cultural life, and literacy as a tool oppressed groups can master and appropriate for their own self-determination. In addition, they were learning to construct their notions of "culture" around the complex, syncretized, lived cultures of real people. So often culture is taught as a static body of beliefs and practices presumed to belong to monolithic, bounded groups. This view is more likely to go unquestioned when curriculum is imposed on children rather than a product of co-construction with them.

Fourth, by connecting students with local political activity, the teacher education program helped them to critique power relations between the community and sectors of the dominant society, recognize various forms of action that groups in the community use to attempt to shift the balance of power, critique the ideology of cultural deprivation many of them began the program with, and learn how they can support ongoing community empowerment efforts. For example, through his work with computers in a community agency, a white student reevaluated his initial assumption that the Black community did not value computer literacy, and realized that people cannot buy computers they cannot afford; he also gained some appreciation of the Black community's use of the computer as a tool for national networking. He subsequently began to ask how computer technology can be made more affordable to low-income communities.

Fifth, from its inception the program had inclusive goals, designed to meet the needs of preservice teachers of color as well as their white counterparts. It purported to go well beyond sensitizing its largely white, female, middle class student body to the "realities" of the inner city. Flexibility, opportunities for linking with others in shifting roles, emphasis on dialogue, co-construction, understanding of multiple perspectives, and so on, provided ample opportunities for students to recognize how schooling could be constructed around the strengths of the community. Central College's approach to service learning provided students opportunities to frame four fundamental questions (Giroux, 1992) regarding the organization of schools, and to seek answers from school personnel as well as students, parents, and grassroots organizations in the communities they serve: (a) What knowledge do we teach? (b) How does this knowledge relate to students' lives, (c) How can students engage with that knowledge? and (d) How does curriculum and pedagogy facilitate individual and group empowerment?

Sixth, the structure and activities of the program enabled students to question the assumption that pedagogical techniques that are advocated within the context of formal schooling can be unproblematically transported to other contexts, such as community youth centers, women's shelters, runaway shelters, and so on. Education in the community differs from school-based education in two important ways. First, it is not structured around lesson plans. Risk, unpredictability, dialogue, and bonding are the words that define education outside of school bureaucracies (Smith, 1994). In fact one of the hallmarks of this program was that it allowed these future teachers to see how curriculum could emerge from social interactions. Second, schools are run by professionals who "invite" students to join a space that has been territorialized and highly regulated by these professionals (Oliveira & Montecinos, in press). In contrast, school professionals do not have a legitimate claim to inhabiting the community centers and other places where education in the community occurs. In these places, the educator's presence is rendered authentic by securing, from the youth, an invitation to be there. The educator has to learn how to gain a space among the many social actors that compete to influence those who are to be educated.

In addition to fostering the political education of these prospective teachers, the type of immersion in community life afforded by Central College opens up the possibility for learning about pedagogical practices that are used by educators who work outside the formal schooling system. Community-based learning, in this way, provides alternative pedagogical frameworks that can be used to help prospective teachers to critique and improve what they are being taught in their teacher education courses. Additionally, by working with educators from the informal sector they can expand their instructional repertoire as they acquire pedagogical knowledge generated by various community educators students encounter. This pedagogical knowledge can, in turn, help teachers build bridges between students' school life and their community life. Prospective teachers' involvement with the community should give them opportunities to figure out how to tap into the "funds of knowledge" that families rely upon in their daily lives (Faltis, 1993; Moll, 1992).

Uncovering the Model of a Proposed Partnership

We offer the following set of questions that can help partners in education critically interrogate the structure and content of the partnership they are seeking to forge. Community-based learning as a part of the multicultural curriculum offers a way of helping teachers learn to engage in partnership models of institution-building. Community-based learning, however, must be carefully constructed, since the dominator context in which we structure these learning activities makes us vulnerable to impose dominator dynamics. 1. To what extent are problems that marginalized communities face viewed as being embedded in the community and its culture, and to what extent are the problems viewed as resulting from power imbalances with the wider society? 2. Is the school's involvement with the community mainly framed as charity work (e.g., helping out "disadvantaged" people) or as addressing the root, systemic causes of issues? 3. How are the needs of various stakeholders' (e.g., the school, the university, the community, students) prioritized in the school-community relationship? 4. How are roles within the school-community project assigned, and by whom? 5. Whose knowledge is considered most worthy of consideration when framing problems and solutions? 6. How is feedback about the school-community project obtained and used? 7. How is conflict among diverse groups understood? 8. How are relationships with the community structured throughout the curriculum?

References

Faltis, C. J. 1993. *Joinfostering: Adapting teaching strategies for the multilingual classroom.* Englewood Cliffs, NJ: Merrill/Prentice-Hall.

Giroux, H. A. 1992. Post-colonial ruptures and democratic possibilities: Multicultural as anti-racist pedagogy. *Cultural Critique* 21, 5-39.

Moll, L. C. 1992. Bilingual classroom studies and community analysis. *Educational Researcher* 21 (2), 20-24.

Montecinos, C. 1994. Teachers of color and multiculturalism. *Equity & Excellence in Education* 27(3), 34-42.

Oliveira, W., and C. Montecinos. In press. Social pedagogy: A matter of presence, commitment, identification, and availability. *Teaching Education.*

Sleeter, C. E. 1993. How White teachers construct race. In C. McCarthy and W. Crichlow (Eds.), *Race, identity, and representation in education* (pp. 167-171). New York: Routledge.

Smith, M. K. 1994. *Local education: community, conversation, praxis.* Buckingham, England: Open University Press.

Partnership in Ministry

Ruthmary Powers

In all of our ministry environments we cannot assume mutuality and partnership even when those words are spoken. After 5,000 years of a dominator culture, many would like to change and work in a collaborative way, but find it easier to fall back to old patterns of behavior. Although we talk "partnership" most of us have had very little experience in our lives of truly mutual and collaborative relationships.

So first we need to identify what behaviors, actions, attitudes in myself and my team (coworkers) move toward a dominator rather than a partnership mentality. How can we move toward being in partnership with one another and those we serve? What are some movements toward partnership?

The questions below are here to begin to work toward partnership with greater clarity and consciousness within the context of theological reflection. The first statement such as "person as other-determined" is a position of the dominator. The movement toward partnership is to have people self-determined.

The remainder of the movements are similar. There is no one way to do this, nor is the listing of movements a final listing. As you attempt to reflect on them you may be able to identify other ways in which you can move toward a partnership environment. Enjoy the journey!

Reflection Questions

Movement from Persons as Other-Determined to Persons as Self-Determined

Who is invisible? Who is not named? Who is spoken about rather than to? When decisions are made, who is consulted? Who makes the final decision? Where is there delegation concerning decision-making?

Movement from Exclusion to Inclusion

How are individuals and groups included in your daily and extraordinary work? How do you know who's been left out? Is there a process to check? What does the staffing look like? What does the altar look like at daily mass, Sunday Liturgy, festive occasions? How can it be made more inclusive? How do you feel about inclusive language/imagery? Do you use it? Insist upon it?

Movement from Ethnocentricity to Cultural Pluralism

Do you find yourself saying, "I'd be happy to have more ____, if only they would ____"? Who provides diversity for your staff? Your parish? Is there an active seeking out of those who may be "different"? How are differences dealt with on your team? In your parish? Are differences seen as growth and learning opportunities?

Movement from Triumphalism and Condescension to Collaboration and Mutuality

What is your attitude toward authority? Do you or the team members need to have all the answers? Are you concerned that individuals and groups are incapable of making decisions for themselves? Do you look at others and find ways in which you are different? Better? How do you define collaboration? Mutuality?

Movement from Win-Lose Mentality to Win-Win Mentality

Do you find a competitive streak in your team or yourself? What kind of language do you use concerning dispute situations? Are you looking to "win" rather than negotiate?

Movement from Isolation to Connection

Who is isolated? How do you know about those who are isolated? What plans or processes are in place to insure connectedness? How do members of the staff feel? Does each member and those employed feel a part of the parish? If someone says they feel isolated, how do you feel inside? How do you react?

Movement from Bewilderment and Confusion to Defining Core Values

Where do you or the staff members feel confused and vague? What kinds of emotions are regularly displayed at staff meetings? If someone were to see you from the outside how would he or she name the values they see you display? Does your mission include a way to evaluate your movements toward partnership action? Can you see movement toward partnership in yourself through reflection and prayer?

Have you and staff members discussed images of partnership/dominator mentalities? Have you or your staff members reflected on ways in which you can move more productively toward working in a partnering way? What obstacles in yourself can you identify? Where do you draw the line in your own movement toward partnership?

Context: Describe your work/parish environment. What stands out that is helpful to partnership or hinders partnership? What is the context in which you work and relate to the team and the people to whom you minister?

Climate: What elements, qualities, characteristics need to be present to create an environment which fosters partnership? (Linking rather than ranking individuals and groups, etc.)

Productivity: What elements contribute to a greater productivity by those involved in the parish/ministerial environment? How do you personally measure productivity?

Challenges: What are some of the challenges that have confronted you as you work toward partnership? How have you met them? Have you been able to work through to a satisfactory conclusion?

Comfort and Critique: What is the general "feeling" at your parish/ministry setting? How is critique handled? Conflict? How are issues that cause conflict addressed? By the group? By individuals?

Metaphor or Image: How would you describe your setting in metaphor or image? How do you visualize it? What can you compare it to? What do the images you evoke tell you about the partnership possibilities in the group?

Exercise on Power

Del Jones

Power is one of the root concepts of cultural transformation theory. So understanding power as seen through the dominator lens and the partnership lens is a core concept. Redefinition of power is one of the toughest applications to overlay on our behavior: the "power over" of the authoritarian, hierarchical dominator model vis à vis the "power with," the power within, shared power of the partnership model.

In this exercise, the group moves into 3 small groups to discuss their power-over experiences in one of these three arenas: worksite, relationship, school/family. At the worksite, discussion usually centers on times when ranking prevailed or when gender was the main issue: the boss makes all the decisions or always chooses the male employees to attend the training classes. In relationships, people usually mention the lack of willingness to share decision-making, the handling of money or cooperate in managing the household. In the school and family, persons remember that when they were children or youth, fear was used as a way to manipulate the person's life.

The facilitator explains that they will have 15 minutes to discuss power as experienced through the dominator lens. When the bell rings (or some agreed to signal), each group will choose the most moving experience and plan a role play showing how this experience could be changed/re-experienced through a partnership lens.

Groups return to the large group and share role plays, followed by discussion of personal experiences through both the dominator and the partnership lenses.

Skits to Understand Gender Roles in Families

Vivian Swearingen

Ask the members of the class to raise their hands to show who grew up in traditional families where their father worked outside the home and their mother was a fulltime mother and housewife, who grew up in a household where both parents worked, and who grew up in a household that doesn't fit in either of these categories (single parent household, changed households while they were growing up, etc.).

Ask the groups to gather in different sections of the room. Ask them to discuss for a certain amount of time what it was like growing up in that type of family, with each group making sure that every person in the group has a chance to describe their experiences. Suggest they create a short skit of a few minutes that demonstrates what it was like growing up in that type of family based on the experiences they had, with one person introducing the characters in the skit at the beginning.

As each skit finishes, ask the class what it was like growing up in that type of family situation, what it felt like, the pros and cons. At the end of the skits, have the class compare the different situations.

The Partnership Way
With Children

Mici Gold

I raised my daughters not to tolerate dominator behavior from adults. Needless to say, I've heard many a time from various adults in their lives! What I often discover about the behavior of these adults is that they expect children to "respect" them without respecting the child in return. For example, they are not above using humiliation to control a child in front of her (or his) peers. Or threatening with bad grades or removal from a team.

As a teacher myself, I know that it would be easier to rely on such tricks — in the short run. I think it backfires in the future, sometimes because we run out of effective threats and always because it does not produce the kind of person we really want to shape. I like to start addressing a behavioral problem in class with a line like, "Hold on, this isn't working well. We have to change something." Or "Someone here is upset. Whatever just happened isn't what we want. What could we do to make it better?" (Incidentally, I avoid asking "what" happened, nor do I permit discussions of it because, in my experience, if it ever leads to solutions, it won't do so quickly enough for children — or often adults, either.)

In class, I consciously alternate calling on a boy and a girl, so that everyone realizes their input is needed and valued. I remind students who have side conversations while a classmate is speaking, that everyone deserves to be heard and I won't let the speaker continue until everyone is listening. And no matter what a student answers to my question, I try to reply in a way that honors his or her effort to participate (not always easy). I don't think I've ever told a student, "You're wrong." Of course, I *do* sometimes have to say, "What did you hear as the question?"

Another way I demonstrate that everyone counts is not to let the more aggressive students (usually, but not always, the boys) dominate the class. For example, I do not reward those who push ahead. When I see a particular pushy group at the front of a line (lines are sometimes still necessary with classes of 30), I walk to the other end of the line, where the students have cooperated to lineup, and let them be first. Silly, but the class soon learns that shoving others around won't get them anywhere. I also let them come up with ways to make sure everyone gets a turn. They come up with some great ideas!

The same aggressive students may receive a lot of praise for their behavior in competition sports, but in the "sports" we do, these students are penalized for crowding out their peers. Often, the quieter, meeker students come up with the best solution for an activity. Not listening to their teammates may cost them time. (Our *only* competition is against time and never another team. The way we enforce that is to have students repeat the activity, after discussing what they could do differently, and seeing whether they can "beat the time" of the first round.) And we honor creative (cooperative) solutions.

Now I admit that these are very little efforts in the total lifetime of a child. But the more of us who do such little things, the sooner we can make changes in the whole world.

THE FEMALE FIGURE IS FROM A GROUP OF THREE WOMEN, PROBABLY PRIESTESSES, KNOWN AS THE "BLUE LADIES." THE MALE FIGURE IS KNOWN EITHER AS THE "YOUNG PRINCE" OR THE "PRIEST KING." THEY DATE BACK TO 1600 B.C. AND CAN BOTH BE SEEN AT THE PALACE IN KNOSSOS, CRETE. PARTICULARLY FASCINATING IS THE MINOAN FEELING FOR LIGHT-HEARTED, HIGH-STYLE FASHIONS THESE FIGURES DISPLAY.

Creative Problem-Solving in the Partnership Paradigm

Sandra Heywood

So many of us know exactly what we need to do to be healthy, to form good habits and relationships, or to accomplish our goals. Nevertheless, often we don't do it or we do it so inconsistently that our results are a perfect example of oscillation: good results one day that fall apart the next. Why do we do this?

Very often our mixed results are the outcome of a reactive stance. We fail to take a creative, rather than reactive approach because we align with negative motivators like needing to lose weight or having to improve our performance in sales or, as an organization, the need to turn around the finances. These motivations typically find us working against ourselves. As our problems diminish, so does our motivation to make changes. Performance then slacks off soon after our motivation does.

By forming a partnership, first with ourselves, we are able to sustain our efforts toward the outcomes we so badly want to create. As we move toward our positive goals, we are encouraged by our progress and want to sustain the effort.

Based on this model of positive motivation, we can do group exercises, sharing our experiences of how we have tried to create certain results in our lives. Most of us, for example, have had experiences with visualization that have created successful outcomes. (E.g., share story of winning the heart marathon.) We need to share these stories with each other to remind ourselves of what works.

After sharing positive results in dyads, a few people share in the large group. Then, back with the original or a new partner, each person shares memory of an effort that failed because the motivator was a negative one, usually based on fear.

The next step is to write out a personal example of oscillation, or inconsistent progress toward a goal. Analyze the driving motivator. Assuming it was fear or the need to change something about oneself, how could this situation have been re-framed to define what it is we want to create? Go around the room with each person contributing one example of a motivation change from negative to positive.

Expand this to show how partnership principles formed with other people can be used for group creation. Have the group come up with examples from organizations where something of value was created through positive motivation that solved an organization's problem. Pay attention to the positive motivators.

These exercises are helpful because they a) repeatedly show the value of positive motivation, b) give people an opportunity to re-frame things that have not worked for them in the past, c) practice, observe and understand the creative process, and d) make the point that true partnership with self must precede partnership with others in organization work.

When used in the context of understanding the creative process, the exercises allow groups to understand that creativity is not something reserved for a special few but is a stance and a WAY of approaching problem-solving that can be learned and practiced by all. It is a way of doing things, not a rare gift reserved for "artsy" people. Themes of interconnectedness and systems thinking should be emphasized throughout the experiential exercises.

What Happened when Teachers Learned about Partnership

Ann Moliver Ruben

During March 1998 ten teachers met with Dr. Ann Moliver Ruben for three hours once a week for four weeks and learned about partnership. The sessions were sponsored by the Teacher Education Center of the Dade County Public Schools. As an incentive, teachers earned 18 Master Points which could be applied to maintain their State of Florida teaching certificate for attending this class called "Combating Gender Inequities" and paid no fee.

There were seven women and three men in the class. Most of them were teachers in the elementary school. They were given a one-page handout of the partnership philosophy written by Riane Eisler. They saw a videotape of Eisler talking about the need for a partnership society and listened to a few of the chapters from her audiotape *The Chalice and the Blade*. They also had a series of group experiences that came from Dr. Ruben's book *Our Teachers Are Crying* that helped create an atmosphere of trust and sharing. Between Week #3 and Week #4, no class meetings were scheduled so that teachers had an opportunity to apply some of what they learned about the partnership philosophy and write a one-page paper on how they applied it in their everyday lives.

Here are some direct quotes from the teachers:

Faye: Before this class I would have never had my sixth-grade class discuss sexism vs. partnership. After my students read a story about Lisa, they were asked to answer the following questions by saying under what circumstances the practice referred to in the story would be or not be sexism. (1) Excluding boys from an after-school sewing circle; (2) Paying girls less than boys to do the same baby-sitting job; (3) Letting all female baby chicks live but killing most males; (4) Holding beauty contests for boys as well as girls. It was a good learning experience for my students and me.

Pushpa: In India, my native country, my marriage was arranged. But my son, Vijay, was able to pick the girl he married. As a result of being in this class, I had a discussion with him about how he should share the household responsibilities with his wife. I don't want Vijay to follow in my husband's footsteps because he has seen his father dominate me. By being in this class I am sure that marriage is a partnership in which partners help and respect each other.

Hayward: As department chairman of social studies, I usually order textbooks for the coming year. This year I decided to use the partnership approach. I included all the teachers in the department to help me select new textbooks. Each teacher was given at least three different textbooks to evaluate and rate them. At the end of two weeks, the teachers met together and discussed the selections. We all agreed on the same books. I have discovered that partnership or shared decisions can work.

Harold: I am now aware that in my classroom the boys tend to be more overt in their remarks and activities and are usually given a greater percentage of attention. I now believe that girls need to be equally challenged for success. I now realize that we need more classes like this for teachers, parents and students which educate equal valuing of the sexes and a general equalitarian social structure.

Patricia: I surveyed 20 male teachers and 20 female teachers in my school about how they saw people with grey hair. I discovered our society views males with grey hair as being one of distinction whereas women who are grey are seen as older and less virile. I shared the results and my colleagues agreed that the standards for aging are much more different for men than for women. This was a good learning experience for me.

Margaret: This class has been a great factor in opening my eyes to the realization that there is still a lot of work to be done. As an educator I will strive toward promoting equality in the classroom. As a woman I will continue to join in the advancement of women in our society.

Marti: As I reviewed some of the materials I use in my preschool class, I came across this song that I taught the children to sing around Thanksgiving:

I'm an Indian brave and strong
I keep busy all day long
Bows and arrows are my toys
I go hunting with the boys
Hi yah, hi yah, hi yah, hi yah!

As a result of this class, I will no longer teach that song to preschoolers.

Dale: I have become aware of my need to promote the partnership style with my students and hopefully they will become aware of it in their daily dealings with people and family. I am learning to become a good partnership role model.

Our Real History

Linda Grover

I have found the following figures to be an effective way to get across the basic message of *The Chalice and the Blade*. They can be drawn on a blackboard or on a large newsprint pad, projected while you talk, or used as handouts.

Figure 1 shows at a glance the big picture, in terms of prehistory and history and female and male. Figure 2 shows where so much of what makes us human really comes from. Figure 3 shows our potential for change.

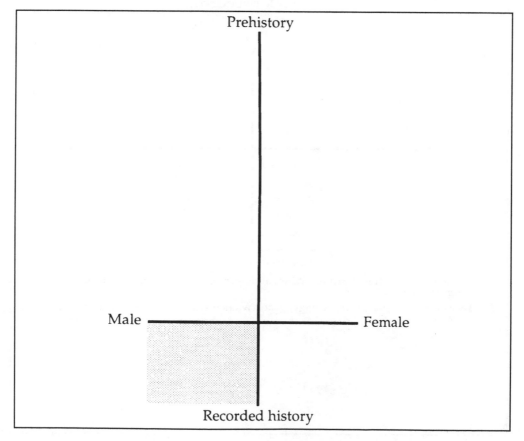

FIGURE 1. HISTORY AS WE LEARNED IT (SHADED AREA)

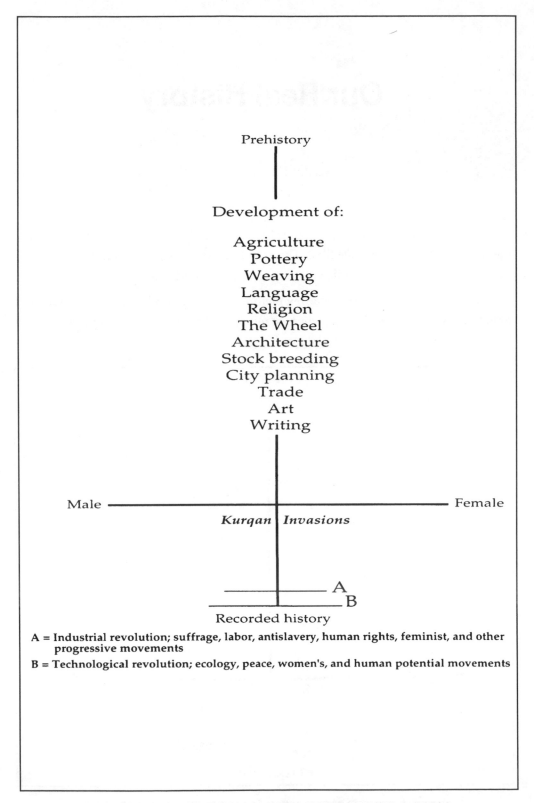

Prehistory

Development of:

Agriculture
Pottery
Weaving
Language
Religion
The Wheel
Architecture
Stock breeding
City planning
Trade
Art
Writing

Male ———————————————————————— Female

Kurgan Invasions

A
B

Recorded history

A = Industrial revolution; suffrage, labor, antislavery, human rights, feminist, and other progressive movements
B = Technological revolution; ecology, peace, women's, and human potential movements

FIGURE 2. WHO REALLY DID WHAT — AND WHEN

Group Juggling

Carol Haag and Jennifer Macleod

This game has been used in training sessions for the Delaware-Raritan Girl Scout Council, Girl Scout troop events, church picnics, peace fairs, etc. It is based on a game reported in More New Games *by Andrew Fluegelman (Garden City NY: Dolphin/Doubleday, 1981).*

This game is something to keep in mind when people say there is no such thing as a noncompetitive game that is enjoyable and also promotes healthful exercise, improves and provides practice in physical and mental skills and coordination, and improves and provides practice in the skills and rewards of cooperative action. Just as long as people don't think that now we've got to have Group Juggling competitive teams, high-pressure coaches, elaborate scoring systems, elimination tournaments, and big prizes for the winners and semi-disgrace for the losers!

Equipment needed: a few people, a few balls (preferably soft), and some space; the game can be adjusted to suit the space available.

Group juggling is a game in which people who may not be able to juggle individually can juggle through cooperating.

Everyone forms a circle and raises one hand. One person (the "initiator") takes a ball and throws it to someone else in the circle. The receiver notes who threw it to her, lowers her raised hand, and throws the ball to another person who has a raised hand. This process continues until everyone in the circle has received the ball at least once and the last throw goes back to the initiator — who continues the process by throwing it to the same person as before.

People should watch the person from whom they receive the ball and then throw it each time to the same person they did in the initial round. If a ball drops, the person nearest to it simply picks it up and throws it to the person to whom she always throws.

Continue for a few rounds, until all is going smoothly. The initiator now adds a second ball. When that is also going smoothly (along with the first), she adds a third ball, and then a fourth — and as many as the group can keep going.

The group can go for

- the highest possible number of balls in the air,

- precision of throwing so none collide in mid-air and escape,

- the most hilarity as balls careen off each other crazily,

- the greatest speed, or

- nothing but the fun of creating something marvelous together.

The game is over when people are laughing too much to throw anything, or when it becomes boring and time for a new game.

The game can be modified for little children by sitting on the floor and rolling large balls — collisions are guaranteed. People who are good throwers can use hard balls and a large outdoor field. Mixed groups or "klutzes" can use Nerf balls, which are easily caught and incapable of injuring even the most unwary receiver.

Partnership Action

A Quick Guide

Gail Van Buuren

Living Partnership

- Actively use partnership in your daily activities and relationships.

- Introduce partnership concepts in your workplace, your club, your family.

Starting Groups

- Plan a partnership evening with friends.

- Start a partnership group in your community.

- Become the facilitator of a workshop or partnership evening using *The Partnership Way* to explore partnership living.

Speaking and Writing

- Speak at meetings, clubs, church groups about any aspect of the transformation from domination to partnership.

- Speak to your schools about textbook updates incorporating a more balanced picture of our past and present.

- Give a guest talk in your child's or friend's classroom.

- Write letters to newspaper and magazine editors, TV and radio stations about the partnership movement; request they cover news everywhere expressing this new orientation to peace, ecology, economics, feminism — and all other aspects of our lives!

Teaching

- Plan to teach a course on partnership — *The Partnership Way* will provide most of what you need to plan curricula.

- Influence others to do the same, particularly friends who are already teaching in schools, colleges, universities, and religious institutions.

Recreating in Partnership

- Find or design cooperative as opposed to competitive games for children and/or adults to play and learn from.

- Create partnership literature for children and adults.

- Communicate the partnership model through your artistic medium.

Sharing *The Chalice and the Blade*

- Give the book as a gift.

- Send a copy to the influential people to whom you have access, including corporation executives, politicians, teachers, ministers, and media people.

- Make sure that the book is available in school and public libraries and bookstores near you.

- Do the same with *The Partnership Way*.

Supporting the Center for Partnership Studies

- When speaking to groups, teaching a course, writing to the media, or just talking to friends and business associates, tell people about the Center for Partnership Studies.

- Do a fundraiser and send us an appropriate share.

- Document what you are doing and send us summaries of what works.

- Let us know what aspects of *The Chalice and the Blade, The Partnership Way*, and the Center for Partnership Studies you find most important and/or useful.

Center for Partnership Studies, Box 51936, Pacific Grove, CA 93950.

Mindfulness Exercises

Ron Kurtz

These are exercises developed by Ron Kurtz, originator of Hakomi Therapy and author of the book by the same title, for a joint workshop he gave with Riane Eisler at Esalen in 1989.

Exercise 1: Mindfulness Fantasy

The following fantasy is led by the facilitator. The purpose is to help participants to experience a clear, calm state of mindfulness to be used in other exercises that require mindfulness.

In a slow, soft voice, the facilitator speaks as follows:

Please allow yourself to come to a calm, quiet space inside yourself. Let the concerns of the day subside for now. As you are relaxing, I would like to guide you with some imagery. Imagine you and me sitting quietly by a still pond deep in a forest on a clear comfortable day. We've been sitting for a long time, silently, without needing to speak. Just being quiet, feeling the air, soft and pleasant against the skin, with the smells of the forest around us. The forest is very still, except for the sounds of an occasional bird and only the slightest movement of the air. The face of the pond is still, the surface, mirrorlike. In that mirror we can see still clouds. Shifting focus, we can look through the mirror seeing the pebbles at the bottom of the pond. As we're sitting, not speaking, you notice a leaf that's being carried by the wind from high in a tree. It's turning slowly, falling gently from the clouds toward the pond. In the pond, another leaf, a mirror leaf, is rising slowly from the bottom, moving toward the surface. The two leaves move together meeting exactly where the water meets the air. They come gently together and at that spot, a small wave ripples out and moves toward the edges of the pond. There, in the shallow water at the edges, the wave embraces the grass, which dances its delight.

Exercise 2: Embodying Partnership

Part 1: Standing in pairs, guided by the facilitator(s), each person goes inside, eyes closed, and one at a time, takes on these three modes of being: (1) equal with others, (2) dominant, (3) victim. (The facilitator says, for example, *Imagine that you are ... equal with others.*)

In each case, the facilitator then guides the participants through noticing posture, breathing, energy flow, comfort or tension, feelings, attitudes, and especially how the body is *being used* by the mode of being.

After each mode has been experienced and studied, participants discuss their experiences with partners. The facilitator waits till discussions seem complete, then asks for questions. After questions, a second part of the exercise begins.

Part 2: In fours (or threes), all people start in neutral (for them). All but one person close their eyes and get mindful. While they have their eyes closed, the remaining person goes into one of the modes of being — equal, dominant, or victim. Others, when ready, open their eyes for a second or so, look at the person doing the mode, and study their automatic reactions to that person. When all are ready, the four discuss their experiences. Repeat the process with different people taking on different modes while the others study how they automatically react. In these studies and discussions, we can discover some of our basic ways of dealing with the issues of partnership (equals) and dominance. Large group discussion can follow, stimulated by these experiences.

The Sensitivity Cycle

Ron Kurtz

Sensitizing ourselves to ourselves and to others involves going through a cycle something like the following:

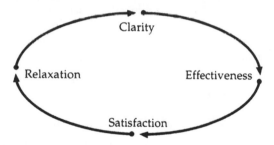

We relax, seeking clarity, effectiveness, and satisfaction.

But along the way are certain barriers we must work through — barriers to insight, response, nourishment, and completion.

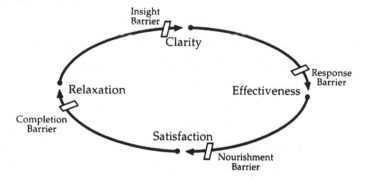

The message of this diagram is that we don't get there all at once. We get there in stages, cycling through these functions and barriers maybe several times before getting where we want to go.

This kind of sensitizing is a vital step in the transition from dominator to partnership living.

The Mondragon Model

Harry Morel

I have heard Riane Eisler mention that we need to learn partnership technology and partnership economics. I have been striving toward that goal for many years and think the natural agricultural system is a special window into partnership technology and economics.

To realize the significance of this relationship, we must remember that civilization is still based on agriculture. For this reason, practicing natural agriculture might further partnership economic thinking.

The idea behind this natural agriculture process, developed by Japanese plant pathologist Masanobu Fukuoka, is to let plants grow without too much restriction, to work in partnership with Mother Nature. Some plants are cut down and others are promoted. The soil is not cut and torn up by plowing, thus avoiding erosion. The top layer of the soil, together with the shredded dead biomass that is returned to the earth, provides the fertilizer and the "placenta" for new growth. Insecticides and fungicides are substituted with knowledge of natural insect and disease cycles.

The Mondragon Cooperatives in the Basque region of Spain, which thirty years ago established the country's fastest-growing bank, the Working People's Bank, have developed a blueprint for a very successful partnership business model that could provide the organizational structure for natural agriculture. In "The Mondragon Experiment" a 45-minute BBC documentary about this venture, a professor from the London School of Economics shows a 100% higher investment efficiency by these worker-owned cooperatives compared with similar corporations. He cites workers living close to their workplace and the trust between management and labor as key factors in the cooperatives' phenomenal productivity.

According to Terry Molner, a partnership business consultant who studied the Mondragon Cooperatives firsthand, a chain of command structure, as seen in stock-holding corporations, is voted into power within a consensus organization in which all members are stockholders and have equal political power. The command structure provides an efficient, coordinated division of labor, yet does not control the organization. The key to this circumstance is that nonworkers are prohibited from owning stock in the company. Since only people who work in the company can own stocks, the command structure remains under the control of the people who are under its control. The circle is complete.

At the general meeting the stockholders set company policy. The directors in the chain of command put this policy into action. The chain of command is a ranked structure in which higher ranks command lower ranks. The command structure itself, however, is organized as a partnership structure in which members are equal in their decision-making and voting power.

In the Mondragon Model, the organizational structure is both pyramidal (ranking) and circular (linking). The top and bottom are connected to form a circular path of power. Ranking serves to identify and utilize people's best talents and capabilities, while linking guarantees freedom and democratic process.

Developing Partnership Skills

An Invitation to the Reader

Jennifer S. Macleod

An essential step in the shift to a partnership mode is to develop partnership skills to substitute for the old dominator skills. This is not easy, because we have so little to draw on. Most of our games, customs, institutions, languages, and rituals are structured (whether consciously or unconsciously) to maintain the dominator mode of relating to other human beings and to the earth and its other forms of life. But there is also a growing body of resources. The issue of how to develop partnership skills has, in one form or another and under a number of different terminologies and with a number of different focuses, been the subject of a number of books. And as we move ahead over the next years and decades, we can hope for hundreds of books and other types of communication, in all languages and in all countries, on the subject.

Creating, Achieving, and Succeeding
Without Dominator-Type "Win-Lose" Competition

In a dominator society, it is generally assumed that we must create strong competition among individuals and groups in order to motivate them to perform well and achieve difficult goals. In schools, students are pitted one against the other (individually or in groups or teams) in the classroom and on the playing fields. From second grade spelling bees to school athletics and "grading on the curve," to professional sports, to getting promoted on the job, to wars between nations, we are taught that we can only truly win if someone else loses. The race goes to the swift, and everyone else "fails."

There is, however, increasing evidence that fostering such competition does not necessarily improve performance or creativity or achievement, that in fact it tends to have negative effects instead. This topic has been explored in depth by Alfie Kohn in his book *No Contest: The Case Against Competition* (Houghton Miffin 1987).

When we begin to think about it, we can see many ways to promote creativity, excellence, and achievement without ever invoking the supposed motivation of beating out someone else. There have always been fine artists and performing artists, creative writers, thinkers, and scientists who have accomplished extraordinary things — individually or with others — without competitiveness ever rearing its head.

In fact, when we think about it, it may become clear that the truly greatest accomplishments have always been those in which beating competitors is not a motivating factor.

Thus, we could profitably examine every aspect of our society to see how we can reduce unnecessary competition — the competition that we have artificially created in order to goad people who would otherwise (we thought) perform poorly and achieve little.

The best strategies for reducing competition will probably not be to try to prohibit or campaign against practices such as spelling bees, educational methods that pit student against student, highly competitive "winning is everything" sports such as Little League baseball and professional football, and so forth. Such strategies are likely to meet with very strong opposition, not only because competitive practices seem natural and inevitable in the current dominator-oriented societal structure, but also because people do not see any satisfactory alternatives.

Instead, better strategies may involve the introduction or promotion and encouragement of well-designed partnership-style activities — games, educational methods, athletics, projects of a variety of kinds — that call for and develop skill in collaboration and cooperation. As these grow and show their value, they will provide attractive alternatives that people will begin to turn to by choice.

At some point, dog-eat-dog competitive activities will be seen to be undesirable, and people will be more willing to give them up because there will be better alternatives clearly visible and already proven effective.

Here, for example, is an experiential exercise that could be used in a workshop setting with a group of from four to about ten people.

The "Making Music" Exercise

Each member of the group is arbitrarily assigned a different simple musical instrument such as an ocarina, a toy piano, a tin flute, a set of drums, a kazoo.

The assignment is a competition to determine which member of the group can produce the best musical performance. Competitiveness is encouraged by the promise of first, second, and third prizes and a congratulatory ceremony.

Each participant then performs for the group and is graded by the trainer on the quality of the music he or she produces, without regard to any other considerations such as effort, difficulty of the particular instrument, or whatever. The prizes are handed out in a ceremony, with the trainer giving warm praise and congratulations to the winners for being "the best."

After a break, the instruments are reassigned, so that each participant is given a different instrument. This time, the assignment is for the group to produce a musical performance of one or more pieces. The new aim is a cooperative one: to produce the best music possible, with no element of competition. There are no prizes, just the potential satisfaction of achievement.

Participants may not switch instruments, but otherwise they are free to organize the effort in any way they see fit. They may if they wish all stay together, or they may break up into smaller groups to prepare separate musical pieces.

The performance should be recorded on audiotape and played back immediately afterward, so that the performers can hear again the music they produced. Then the group discusses and compares the two experiences, their feelings about the exercise and about each other, and the nature and quality of the music produced.

The expectation, of course, is that the collaborative second assignment will not only be a far more effective and enjoyable learning experience, promoting understanding and appreciation as well as musical skill among the participants, but will also result in an obviously better quality of musical performance.

An exercise like this one would not have to be limited to an artistic effort such as music making. For example, a similar design could be used in which the assignment is to solve puzzles, such as the familiar puzzles in which the goal is to separate two or more entangled pieces of twisted rigid metal tubing.

The discussion that follows the experience would, as with the music exercise, compare the experience of each assignment — and the quality of the work accomplished. In all probability, the collaborative approach would result in more of the puzzles being solved more quickly, more learning of what strategies are most effective in solving puzzles of this type, and better communications and relationships among those involved.

Achieving Win-Win Results in Conflict Situations

One of the underlying assumptions in a dominator society is that when two parties (individuals or groups) are in conflict with one another, the only possible outcomes are

- a continuation of the conflict, so that neither party has what it wants (a lose-lose situation)

- a resolution in which one side prevails and gets what it wants, while the other side fails (a win-lose resolution)

- a compromise, in which each side gets only some of what it wants (This could be termed a lose-lose resolution, even though the two "lose" situations may be some improvement over the earlier situation).

There is, however, a fourth possible outcome: a win-win resolution, in which *both* sides achieve the major elements of what they seek. This is a creative solution, often something that neither side even conceived of until they worked together on the challenge of finding such a solution and thus satisfying the needs of both. This type of solution is obviously by far the best possible outcome, yet we, brought up in a dominator society, are often ill-equipped to even conceive that such a solution is possible.

The reader who would like to explore the concepts and strategies of negotiation (conflict resolution) that creates solutions or agreements that meet the most important needs and desires of both parties may want to read Roger Fisher and William Ury, *Getting to Yes: Negotiating Agreement Without Giving In* (Penguin Books 1983) and Roger Fisher and Scott Brown's more recent *Getting Together: Building Relationships* (Houghton Miffin 1988).

Creating and Sustaining Effective, Successful Organizations and Institutions Without Dominator Hierarchies

We are all very familiar with hierarchical institutions and organizations, from the family to the largest corporations and governments; and the hierarchies are based on domination by those with power over the others. In the dominator model, this is inevitable.

But if we are to develop societies and cultures on the partnership model, we will have to (and will want to) have institutions and organizations that are modeled not on dominator hierarchies, but on cooperation and collaboration instead.

This is a very tall order. While we may be able to see ways to decrease destructive competition, and to conduct negotiations in win-win ways, we may currently know and understand far less about how to create organizations/institutions on the partnership model. For doesn't the elimination of the dominator hierarchy mean anarchy, chaos, and an organization that has no structure — and no effectiveness — whatever?

In fact, there are some important signposts to other ways. Non-hierarchical (not based on a dominator hierarchy) does not mean structureless. Nor does it mean that everyone has to be paid the same or do the same thing, nor that all tasks — including managing — are rotated among everyone.

What it *can* mean is that all individuals in an organization are there by choice, and take part in decisions as to what role they play, how they work together, and how the work and the organization are structured. The glue that binds the organization together is the common goal, which each individual freely chooses to make one of her or his personal goals as well. Leaders may (and usually will) exist, but they emerge by virtue of their expertise and, particularly, their ability to inspire and help others to work well together for common goals.

Within the discipline of management training, many experiential exercises have been found useful in helping people understand and develop skills in organizing and working in collaborative ways without the power hierarchies of bosses and subordinates.

For example, workshop participants can be given materials such as foam board, rulers and T-squares, cutting equipment, glue and tape, and be given the assignment of building something such as a model house within a tight time schedule. They then organize themselves for the task along whatever lines they choose.

If such an exercise is videotaped, participants learn a great deal about what works well and what doesn't work well in cooperative projects. If the same group is then given another (different) assignment, they usually work better the second time, differentiating roles and cooperating and sharing more effectively, and producing a better result more efficiently.

Small group cooperation in workshops is, of course, a far cry from effective partnership structures for bigger ongoing organizations. It remains exceedingly difficult for organizations, even if they started along partnership lines, to sustain such patterns when surrounded by a larger society and culture that is determinedly and oppressively "dominator" in style.

Reason for optimism exists, however. As people make the effort, and as some succeed in creating and sustaining small and then larger organizations on the partnership model, their success and high performance and achievement will begin to be noticed, and others will become interested in trying the new approaches.

For example, William L. Gore, in his article "The Lattice Organization: A Philosophy of Enterprise" (*Networking Journal* Spring/Summer 1985), describes an organizational structure based on the lattice, in which each person interacts directly with every other person with no intermediary. There is only "natural" leadership — no assigned or assumed authority. This, he says, can be an extremely effective structure in organizations small enough so that everyone knows everyone else.

In organizations larger than that, the challenge is greater — but not impossible to meet. For example, Charles F. Kiefer and Peter M. Senge, in their monograph *Metanoic Organizations: Experiments in Organizational Innovation* (Innovation Associates 1982), describe an approach to larger-scale organizational structure in line with the partnership model.

They call such organizations "metanoic," from the Greek word *metanoia*, meaning a fundamental shift of mind *(meta*, transcending; *noia*, mind). These organizations are based upon the development of a powerful vision and purpose — something that everyone in or attracted to the organization is inspired by and becomes aligned with, so that all involved take full shared responsibility for the success of the whole. In such an organization, there can be tremendous flexibility and creativity in structure, roles, functions — and results far beyond usual expectations.

This approach, say Kiefer and Senge, has brought striking success to a number of actual companies. The Basque cooperatives in Spain, for example, have much to show us. (See "The Mondragon Model" earlier in this section.) These and other groups, such as the Bahai'i and the Quakers, have created structures that have required them to develop partnership skills, and we can learn from these pioneers in partnership development and practical application.

Re-Membering and Re-Entering

Karen-Elise Clay

Re-membering Our Childhood:
The Self and the Earth

(Allow approximately thirty minutes for this discussion exercise.)

Childhood is a time of vulnerability, learning, and growth. Each of us learned different things from our parents and society connected with our gender.

Break into small groups and discuss any or all of the following questions.

1. What did you feel about being raised a female/male?

2. What limitations were placed on you because you were female/male?

3. What was your experience with the educational system?

4. What messages did you receive about your femaleness or maleness from your religion?

5. What adult models did you have?

6. What was your experience in the home — mother, other siblings?

7. Did you limit yourself because of your sex?

After twenty minutes, come together in a large group and ask each small group to share some of the highlights from the experience.

Re-entering:
Moving Toward Personal and Planetary Action

(Allow approximately thirty minutes for this exercise.)

Break into groups of two to four and create a role play using the partnership model to respond to one of the following situations, or create your own situation.

1. Your teenage daughter comes home an hour after curfew, a curfew to which you had mutually agreed. You ...

2. Your husband, who is the sole support of the family, comes home tired and distraught. He tells you he cannot continue at his present job. You …

3. The teacher of your ten-year-old son calls you to say your son has not been completing his homework and is a frequent disruption in the class. You …

4. As the mother of a young child you feel resentment building toward your husband for not contributing more to help with housework and child care. You …

5. Your roommate continually leaves "messes" in the kitchen area, even after you have requested her respect for mutual living space. You …

Closing

To close this session, the facilitator reads aloud: "In this moment we are joined to share thoughts, feelings, and hopes for the future, individually and together. Let us weave tomorrow from our dreams of love and wisdom in partnership with all of life on Earth."

Ideas for Workshops, Topics, and Exercises

Marsha Utain and Arthur Melville

These ideas for discussions, exercises, and workshops are based on these readings: *The Chalice and the Blade* by Riane Eisler; *Bradshaw on the Family* by John Bradshaw (chapters 1-3); "The Drama Triangle and the Emotion Diamond" in *Stepping Out of Chaos* by Marsha Utain; and *Scream Louder* by Marsha Utain and Barbara Oliver.

An easy way to get started is to ask participants to share what in the readings has been most important or meaningful and most distressing or difficult for them.

Discussion Topics

1. To focus on family structure and its influence on our lives:

- List various ways the hierarchical family structure feeds and is part of the dominator model.

- List various covert and overt family rules that set the context for you to be a part of the dominator model.

- Rewrite the family rules. Write a letter to your inner child telling the child that it is no longer necessary for the child to obey the old rules. Also imagine the child in front of you and talk to the child. Let the child write back to you or talk with you.

- Do some emotional healing work with the inner child. Spend time listening to the inner child tell you how difficult it was growing up in a dominator-model family.

2. We need to distinguish between spirituality and religion. Most of us were raised in our families in dominator models of religion. To discover and change those models:

- Write down a list of your religious beliefs.

- Write down who taught them to you, when, and how.

- Notice if fear was involved in the teaching process.

- Notice if fear or compulsion or rigidity or retribution is involved in the practice of religion.

- Take your list, place it on a chair opposite you, imagine the people in your life who gave you your beliefs, and give them back their beliefs.

- Start a new list and place on it what you want and need from a Higher Power and a religion.

- Use beliefs that are nurturing and supportive.

- Recognize your Higher Power as a Being of love, support, creativity, generosity, nurturance, guidance, rather than .punishment, destruction.

- Remember a time when you were very small and felt close to nature.

- Write a fairy tale or story about a child and nature with a loving, supportive environment.

- Spend time in nature. Be aware of the life within the plants and animals around you.

3. To operate in a healthy partnership way, communications, both personal and societal, must be direct, clear, and honest. To focus on communications:

- Write out clear, honest, direct communications to the people in your life with whom you feel incomplete. Practice in your partnership group or with a safe friend. Then send the communications to the people for whom they were originally intended. Notice if you are afraid to do this. If so, you may be dealing with a person who knows only the dominator model.

- Expose rules of secrecy in your family in a safe environment.

- Discover and list the secrets in your family of origin. If you are comfortable with this, share them with friends in a safe environment.

- Discover and list the rules that kept the secrets. Write down who created the rules and how the rules protected them.

4. Agreements that mutually support people are important in a partnership world. Making agreements is necessary when we have different needs and desires.

- Learn how to make agreements and understand the need for agreements in a partnership world. Agreements are specific. The terms are well defined; they are acceptable to all parties involved. Failure to meet the terms of the agreement is dealt with as part of the agreement.

- Learn how to negotiate agreements. Recognize that you must do that prior to the end of the term of the agreement.

5. How do men move from the present archetypes of the dominator model to new archetypes of the partnership model? (See "Getting Started" in Session 4.)

- Write a new story with partnership male archetypes. Share it with people of both sexes. Get honest feedback about what the archetype promote.

- Write new fairy tales for children using the partnership male models and archetypes. Share them with people of both sexes. Get honest feedback about what the models and archetype promote.

- Write poetry for all age groups using the partnership male models and archetypes. Share it with people of both sexes. Get honest feedback about what the models and archetype promote.

- Create artwork for all the above.

6. How do women move from the present archetypes of the dominator model to the new archetypes of the partnership model? (See "Getting Started" in Session 4.)

- Write a new story with partnership female archetypes. Share it with people of both sexes. Get honest feedback about what the archetype promotes.

- Write new fairy tales for children using the partnership female models. Share them with people of both sexes. Get honest feedback about what the model and archetype promote.

- Write poetry for all age groups using the partnership female models and archetypes. Share it with people of both sexes. Get honest feedback about what the models and archetype promote.

- Create artwork for all the above.

Partnership
Resources

THESE WHIMSICAL FIGURES TELL US MUCH OF BOTH THE MINOAN CRETE SENSE OF
HUMOR AND — IN MARKED CONTRAST TO WHAT COMES LATER — A
COMFORTABLE, NONFEARING ATTITUDE TOWARD DEITY. THEY ARE FROM A
MINOAN PLATE FOUND IN THE OLD PALACE OF PHAISTOS, DATING TO 1800 B.C.,
THAT MAKES USE OF ONE OF MANY EPIPHANIES OF THE GREAT GODDESS,
IDENTIFIED BY MARIJA GIMBUTAS AS THE "BEE GODDESS." IN THIS CASE WE HAVE
WHAT SEEMS TO BE TWO BEE PRIESTESSES HOVERING ABOUT WHAT
APPEARS TO BE THE HIVE AS GODDESS.
LINE DRAWING BY JEFF HELWIG FROM THE ORIGINAL.

Partnership and
Dominator Models
Basic Configurations

The table and diagrams that follow give a bird's-eye view of the three key components of the partnership and dominator models. They are useful as a quick introduction to systems thinking about society.

A Comparison of the Three Basic Components of the Dominator and the Partnership Models

Component	Dominator Model	Partnership Model
Gender Relations	The ranking of the male over the female, as well as the higher valuing of the traits and social values stereotypically associated with "masculinity" rather than "femininity"	Equal valuing of the sexes as well as of "femininity" and "masculinity," or a sexually equalitarian social and ideological structure
Violence	A high degree of institutionalized social violence, including wife beating, rape, and warfare, with violence a structural component of the system	A low degree of social violence, with violence, including wife beating, rape, and warfare, not a structural component of the system
Social Structures	A generally hierarchic and authoritarian social organization, with the degree of authoritarianism and hierarchism roughly corresponding to the degree of male dominance	A generally equalitarian social structure

As used in the table above, *masculinity* and *femininity* refer to the dominator stereotypes that associate "real" men with aggression, heroic violence, lack of feeling, and other "hard" traits, and only women with "soft" traits like caring, nonviolence, and compassion. Clearly, there are many caring and compassionate men; and women, as well as men, are capable of violent and uncaring behavior. We want to stress this important distinction, as well as the point that in a partnership model of society, *femininity* and *masculinity* would have different meanings.

Further, the term *hierarchic* refers to what we may call a *domination* hierarchy, or the type of hierarchy inherent in a dominator model of social organization, based on force or the threat of force. Such hierarchies should be distinguished from a second type of hierarchy, which for clarity can be called an *actualization* hierarchy—for example, of molecules, cells, and organs in the body: a progression toward a higher and more complex level of functioning.

The following diagrams indicate how the relationships between the three major components of the two models are interactive, with all three mutually reinforcing one another.

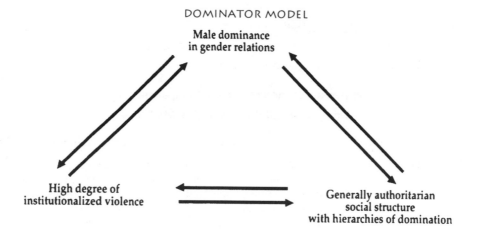

DOMINATOR MODEL

Male dominance
in gender relations

High degree of
institutionalized violence

Generally authoritarian
social structure
with hierarchies of domination

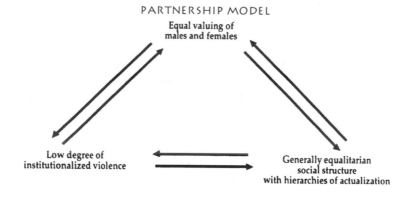

PARTNERSHIP MODEL

Equal valuing of
males and females

Low degree of
institutionalized violence

Generally equalitarian
social structure
with hierarchies of actualization

Seven Basic, Interactive, and Mutually Supporting Differences

The Partnership and Dominator Models

Component	Dominator Model	Partnership Model
Gender Relations	The male is ranked over the female, and the traits and social values stereotypically associated with "masculinity" are valued more highly than those associated with "femininity."	Females and males are equally valued in the governing ideology, and stereotypically "feminine" values, such as nurturance and nonviolence, can be given operational primacy.
Violence	A high degree of social violence and abuse is institutionalized, ranging from wife- and child-beating, rape, and warfare to psychological abuse by "superiors" in the family, the work place, and society at large.	Violence and abuse are not structural components of the system, so that both boys and girls can be taught nonviolent conflict resolution. Accordingly, there is a low degree of social violence.
Social Structure	The social structure is predominantly hierarchic and authoritarian, with the degree of authoritarianism and hierarchism roughly corresponding to the degree of male dominance.	The social structure is more generally egalitarian, with difference (be it based on gender, race, religion, sexual preference, or belief system) not automatically associated with superior or inferior social and/or economic status.
Sexuality	Coercion is a major element in mate selection, sexual intercourse, and procreation, with the erotization of dominance and/or the repression of erotic pleasure through fear. Primary functions of sex are male procreation and male sexual release.	Mutual respect and freedom of choice for both females and males are characteristic of mate selection, sexual intercourse, and procreation. Primary functions of sex are the bonding between the female and male through the give and take of mutual pleasure, and the reproduction of species.

Spirituality	Man and spirituality are ranked over woman and nature, justifying their domination and exploitation. The powers that govern the universe are imaged as punitive entities, be it as a detached father whose orders must be obeyed on pain of terrible punishments, a cruel mother, or demons and monsters who delight in arbitrarily tormenting humans, and hence must be placated.	The spiritual dimension of both woman's and nature's life-giving and sustaining powers is recognized and highly valued, as are these powers in men. Spirituality is linked with empathy and equity, and the divine is imaged through myths and symbols of unconditional love.
Pleasure and Pain	The infliction or threat of pain is integral to systems maintenance. The pleasures of touch in both sexual and parent-child relations are associated with domination and submission, and thus also with pain, be it in the so-called carnal love of sex or in submission to a "loving" deity. The infliction and/or suffering of pain are sacralized.	Human relations are held together more by pleasure bonds than fear of pain. The pleasures of caring behaviors are socially supported, and pleasure is associated with empathy for others. Caretaking, love-making, and other activities that give pleasure are considered sacred.
Power and Love	The highest power is the power to dominate and destroy, symbolized since remote antiquity by the lethal power of the blade. "Love" and "passion" are frequently used to justify violent and abusive actions by those who dominate, as in the kiling of women by men when they suspect them of sexual independence, or in "holy wars" said to be waged out of love for a deity that demands obeisance from all.	The highest power is the power to give, nurture, and illuminate life, symbolized since remote antiquity by the holy chalice or grail. Love is recognized as the highest expresion of the evolution of life on our planet, as well as the universal unifying power.

Table Notes

This table is reprinted from Eisler, *Sacred Pleasure*, pp. 403-405.

The terms *femininity* and *masculinity* as used here correspond to the sexual stereotypes socially constructed for a dominator society (where masculinity is equated with dominance and conquest, and femininity with passivity and submissiveness) and not to any inherent female or male traits.

As used her, the term *hierarchic* refers to what we may call a *domination* hierarchy, or the type of hierarchy inherent in a dominator model of social organization, based on fear and the threat of pain. Such hierarchies should be distinguished from a second type of hierarchy, which may be called an *actualization* hierarchy. An example from biology is the hierarchy of molecules, cells, and organisms in the body: a progression toward a higher and more complex level of function. In social systems, hierarchies of actualization go along with the equation of power with the power to create and to elicit from oneself and others our highest potentials.

The Partnership and Dominator Models

How to Recognize Them when You See Them and Move Toward a Less Tense, More Fulfilling Life

Many of us are trying to change patterns that cause us pain and hold back our personal and social development. To do this, we are trying to identify what we want to hang on to and what we want to leave behind. It is a question, so to speak, of not throwing out the baby with the bath water. Where and how do we draw the line?

This is where the partnership and dominator models can be such effective tools for the liberation of our minds. When we use these models to identify what is going on in every area of our lives, we begin to say to ourselves things like, "That is a dominator belief, attitude, behavior, or process — and I want no more of it," or "This is a partnership belief, attitude, behavior, or process — and this is the way I want to be." By developing and using these basic tools — and this basic way of thinking about everything in our lives — we create key building blocks for the partnership future.

The two tables that follow show some of the main differences between the partnership and dominator models. The first table presents some of the differences between the partnership and dominator models that can be summarized in a single word or phrase. The second table explores some of the more complex and subtle differences.

While differentiation is one of our most important thinking and learning tools, it is important to keep in mind that sometimes the differences between how these two models are manifested in actual practice is a question of degree or emphasis. And some of the contrasts that may initially come to mind, such as the idea that cooperation is only a partnership trait and competition is found only in dominator systems, are too simplistic — and thus not helpful.

There *is* cooperation in the dominator model. A notable example is the cooperation of groups of men to conquer and/or suppress others, be they a modern army or the inquisitors of the Middle Ages. But as the second table indicates, it is a cooperation founded on fear and aggression toward an "out-group."

Similarly, there *is* competition in the partnership model. But in contrast to competition in the dominator model, it is not the exploitive "dog-eat-dog" competition where our natural human capacity tor empathy has been insensitized by dominator socialization (as has particularly been the ease in the upbringing of men). It is a different kind of competition: achievement-oriented rather than winning-oriented, modulated and regulated by feelings of empathy with others rather than by a drive to suppress and conquer others at any cost (as expressed in the well-known adage "all's fair in love and war").

Moreover, while a basic difference between a dominator and a partnership society is that the first is held together primarily by fear and the second by trust, this is not to say that even in a society that approaches very closely the partnership model, we would never be afraid or mistrustful. The difference — and it is major — is that in a dominator society, fear is systematically inculcated in us and trust (beginning with the trust between the female and male halves of humanity) is systematically undermined through dominator cultural myths and social institutions.

This leads to a very important point: the partnership society is *not* a utopian, ideal society free of problems, conflicts, disappointments, or grief. Conflict is a natural aspect of life, as different organisms with different needs, purposes, and plans come together. Grief and disappointment are also inherent in life, if only because we must all die.

The difference — and again it is a major one — lies in how we are taught to deal with these givens. For example, in the dominator model, conflict is emphasized, but at the same time the violent suppression of conflict is institutionalized, and might is equated with right. By contrast, in the partnership model, conflict is openly recognized, and dealing with it creatively in ways where both parties learn and grow is encouraged.

Another important point to stress is that the difference between partnership and dominator beliefs, attitudes, behaviors, and processes is not a matter of "us" versus "them," for as Walt Kelly's Pogo said, "I have met the enemy and he is us." Both models operate within each of us.

In some of us the dominator model runs rampant. In others the partnership model is afraid to emerge except in wholly protected circumstances. In still others the partnership model is already quite strong. But every one of us faces the challenge of creating for ourselves new habits of thinking, feeling, and acting — habits appropriate for a world where we can live more harmoniously with one another and our natural habitat. This is why knowing what the dominator model is, where it came from, how it operates within us and upon us, and what to do about it — and knowing what the partnership model is, where it came from, how it operates within us and upon us, and how to use it — is of central importance in this time of confusion. Recognizing the models is essential for our own clarity and for human advancement.

In all these charts there is room for you to add your ideas. We invite you to send the best of these to us at the Center for Partnership Studies, 51936, Pacific Grove, CA 93950.

Key Words Comparison of the Dominator and Partnership Models	
Dominator Model	Partnership Model
Fear	Trust
Win/lose orientation	Win/win orientation
Power over	Power to/with
Male dominance	Gender partnership
Sadomasochism	Mutual pleasure
Control	Nurture
Ranking	Linking
One-sided benefit	Mutual benefit
Manipulation	Open communication
Destruction	Actualization
Hoarding	Sharing
Codependency	Interdependency
Left-brain thinking	Whole-brain thinking
Negative conditioning	Positive conditioning
Violence against others	Empathy with others
Taking orders	Working in teams
Alienation	Integration
Nuclear arms race	International partnership
War	Peace
Secrecy	Openness/accountability
Coercion	Participation
Indoctrination	Education
Conquest of nature	Respect for nature
Conformity	Creativity

Key Concepts Comparison of the Dominator and Partnership Models

Dominator Model	Partnership Model
Arbitrary freedom for a few	Empathetic freedom for everyone
Those who are different seen as inferior	Celebration of diversity
Women and men seen as opposites in "war of sexes"	Men and women seen as human beings who are different but not inferior or superior
Masculinity[1] equated with domination and femininity with submission	Masculinity and femininity seen as having both active and passive components
"Masculine" values such as conquest and domination given precedence	"Feminine" values such as caring and nonviolence given precedence
High degree of violence, ranging from rape, child abuse, and wife battering to war, modeled through sacred and secular images to maintain force-based rankings	Linking as primary principle of organization manifested in images that celebrate life-giving, life-maintaining, and life-enhancing activities
Male images of heroic violence institutionalized and sanctified	Male images of gentle nurturance honored
Chronic hatred and fear systematically inculcated	Chronic hatred and fear recognized as outcome of an imbalanced social and ideological system; trust (between races, countries, women and men) supported through ideology and institutions
Violence and sexual conquest idealized at the same time that law and order are touted as central to social control	Violence is seen for what it is and mutual respect rather than control are central to concepts of law and order
Femininity portrayed as indirect and manipulative, and devalued	Femininity portrayed as creative and nurturing, and honored.
Inventiveness by a few men supported to maintain the dominator system (as in ever "better" weapons and fear-instilling images and myths)	Creativity by everyone supported to actualize both women's and men's higher individual and social potentials
Woman imaged as idealized virgin/mother or dishonored witch/whore, primarily as relational to a man	Woman imaged as full-fledged human being, neither vilified nor idealized, powerful in her own right, both spiritually and temporally
Leader as a man (and occasional woman) who gives orders to subordinates or followers	Leader as a woman or man who inspires others to work for commonly agreed-on goals
Conquest/exploitation-oriented, insensitive competition	Achievement-oriented, empathetic competition
Conflict is emphasized, but at the same time the violent suppression of conflict through "winning" and "conquest" is encouraged — in fact, idealized	Conflict is recognized as natural among different individuals with different needs and desires, but the peaceful resolution of conflict through win/win approaches is encouraged
People treated as means	People treated as ends

Key Concepts Comparison of the Dominator and Partnership Models

Dominator Model	Partnership Model
Fear and scarcity seen as key motivations for worker productivity	Satisfaction from participation in decision making and sharing in profits and other benefits seen as key motivations for productivity
Manager seen as a controller or cop who gives orders that others follow unquestioningly	Manager seen as one who inspires and encourages participation in production by working teams
Planning is short-term with little thought for future generations	Planning also entails long-term concern for present and future generations
Artificial scarcity is created through war and waste to maintain an exploitive economics and politics of fear	Abundance is jointly created and shared, with the highest value given to the caring work that keeps society going
Quantity of possessions substituted for satisfying human relations	Quality of human relations and material goods emphasized
Domination or power-over becomes an addiction, along with addiction to abusive relationships and harmful substances as means of escaping chronic stress	Mutual support and satisfaction provide a basic sense of self-esteem, leading to interdependency rather than codependency
Selected parts of the social and ecological system focused on, resulting in chronic imbalances in perception and action	Holistic or systems thinking encouraged, resulting in more balanced ways of perceiving the world and living in it.
Society seen as a stable machine with people as expendable cogs	Society viewed as an adaptive structure with people as involved cocreators
The Earth imaged as an object to be conquered and exploited	The Earth imaged as a living organism of which we are a part

1. As used here, *masculinity* and *femininity* refer to the dominator stereotypes that associate "real" men with aggression, heroic violence, lack of feeling, and other "hard" traits, and only women with "soft" traits like caring, nonviolence, and compassion. Clearly, there are many caring and compassionate men; and women, as well as men, are capable of violent and uncaring behavior. We want to stress this important distinction, as well as the point that in a partnership model of society, *femininity* and *masculinity* would have different meanings.

Everyday Partnership Action Chart

This chart, the creation of Robin Van Doren, is a personal tool for partnership action in our everyday lives. It is designed to serve as a partnership agreement with ourselves, clearly setting forth the changes we want to make in key areas of our lives, such as taking better care of our physical and mental health; relationships with our parents, children, friends, lovers, and/or spouses; our work relations; our community participation; the spiritual or religious dimension of our life; our involvement in politics, education, economics, the arts, the media, and other key areas of society.

It is a chart for you to use to meet your particular needs. We have started it off with a few examples that may or may not be relevant for you. Its main purpose is to help you formulate your own partnership agenda and specific ways for turning it into action.

The examples come from many different areas. You could take any one and develop a much more specific agenda. The main thing we have tried to do here is to emphasize personal involvement and responsibility, the "everydayness" of the partnership way, and the importance of committing to doable action. Like New Year's resolutions, these promises to ourselves must be kept in the realm of the possible. Forming a support group to offer feedback and share progress reports will also help, as we work to make these important changes.

While this is your own private chart, it is also a tool for participatory action research. So please send us your best and most practical action-oriented ideas (those that really work for you) and we will try to share them with others through the Center for Partnership Studies.

Everyday Partnership Action Chart

The Dominator Way	The Partnership Way	Action
The way I did it in the past	The way I want to do it now	Changes to make
Ordered my children around	Explain things to my children and enlist their cooperation	Plan time together with my family to work out shared responsibility
Feared those in positions of authority	Respect authority (in the original Latin sense of the word *auctoritas*, or the source of production and invention) in myself and others	Ask questions when needed. Take responsibility for my decisions and actions. Say "no" to actions that violate my integrity or the integrity of others. Find the "common ground."
Deferred totally to external medical advice	Discover the wisdom of partnering my body	Change to healthier eating patterns. Allow time for relaxation. Notice changes that occur and modify actions on the basis of these changes.
Ignored the environmental impact of what I did	Make myself a responsible partner with the environment	Recycle newspapers, cans, bottles, and other used things. Work for legislation that stops or prevents exploitation of environment.
Watched TV and movies that depict violence, greed, and exploitation	Watch media that support partnership and caring	Look for programs and movies that support partnership. Write to TV channels to support these programs. Make lists of good programming available to schools, libraries, and others and share this information. Work on local, national, and/or international media to print and broadcast more partnership images, stories, documentaries, and news. Create images and stories that support partnership.

The Language of Partnership

In trying to shift from a dominator to a partnership way of thinking and living, a major obstacle is our language. How can we think and live as partners if the words in our heads keep reinforcing dominator stereotypes?

Words have a powerful effect on how we think and act. For example, Eskimos have a number of different words for snow, enabling them to distinguish between various conditions others simply see as one. This is an example of how words shape the way we see the world. The use of words like boy to address a grown man in both the American South and many Asian and African colonies is an example of how words serve to define people as inferior, thereby helping to maintain them in a subordinate position. When strangers call grown women "girls" or address them as "dear" or "honey," they are conveying a similarly patronizing message.

The semantics of power relations are particularly striking in the use of words that serve to define the relationship of women and men. In English, for example, the ostensibly generic use of words like *mankind, man,* and *he* to include both sexes unconsciously conditions both women and men to think in male-centered ways, effectively teaching us that women are secondary or do not count. Similarly, words like *chairman* or *congressman* teach us to associate only men with positions of power, effectively discouraging women from aspiring to such positions, except in "exceptional" cases. The use of words like *emasculate* or *effeminate* to express negative meanings further teaches us to value men and "masculinity" over women and anything associated with "femininity."

Today, as the equal value and equal rights of *all* people are increasingly asserted, changes in language are also being recognized as important steps toward the creation of a just society. But these changes are not easy to make. Because linguistic habits are established very early in life, it is difficult to break them. Moreover, languages that are the product of male-dominated societies tend to lack words that express a different world view.

The following terms already in common usage are a few suggestions for those who want to break out of the prison of words that unconsciously force us to think of one half of humanity as less valuable than the other.

Dominator Language	Partnership Language
mankind	humanity/humankind
man	human
he	she or he/one/they
chairman	chairperson/chair
congressman	congressperson
man hours	work hours
manpower	work power, work force
to man	to staff
gentlemen	ladies and gentlemen
Dear Sir	Dear Madam and Sir/Dear Sir or Madam/Dear Madam or Sir/Dear Manager
emasculated	weak /nonassertive
effeminate	decadent/weak
statesman	diplomat/leader/policymaker
sissy	sensitive boy
brotherhood	community/kinship/friendship/unity/partnership
craftsman	artisan/skilled worker
spokesman	speaker/spokesperson/representative
common man	average person

Speaking Our Peace

Teaching the Language of Partnership

Lethea F. Erz

The Challenge of Language

"Saying is believing." Language both shapes and reflects consciousness, revealing a culture's deepest beliefs and values. It's very hard to talk about concepts for which we have no vocabulary. And the words we do have determine how we think about the people, ideas, and phenomena those words describe.

If we hope to create a truly new paradigm based on partnership thinking, it's vital that we be aware of the underlying messages in the very words and metaphors we use to express our thoughts. If we don't, our good intentions may be undermined by the language we use to state them.

The Issue of Inclusion

At this point in time, few people will fail to notice the inappropriate use of "mankind" when what is really meant is "humankind" — both women and men. Most of the old "male-generic" nouns — which supposedly included women but in fact rarely did — have been replaced by neutral descriptors: "people," "firefighters," "mail carriers,""salesfolk," "committee chair," "crew working," and so on.

The Problem of Pronouns

Most people are now aware of alternatives such as "s/he," "she or he" (used equally with "he or she"), and the singular "they/them/their" which is gradually reclaiming grammatical legitimacy as a non-sexist alternative to gendered pronouns. Direct address ("you/your") and the inclusive "we/our" are also useful in many situations.

The Colors of Racism

It's important to examine language that implies something evil about "darkness" or "blackness." Even when used without conscious racist intent, such terms as "black-hearted villain" or "deep dark secret," contrasted with "white knight" or "innocent white lie," contribute to the fear and demonization of dark-skinned people. It's important to consider that in many ancient cultures, black was celebrated as the color of the rich fertile earth, while the *white* color of bones was associated with death.

The Healing Metaphor

Sexism, racism, and other forms of inequality and oppression stem from conflict, with the winners dominating the losers. People are divided into groups labeled "us" and "other." A major goal of *partnership* is moving from this "either/or" thinking to "both/and" conflict-resolution.

Yet many of our everyday expressions perpetuate the dualism of "either/or." These include metaphors of combat and warfare, which in addition to asserting that one side must win and the other lose, also imply that violence is an acceptable way of dealing with challenges.

When politicians launch a "war against crime" they are merely attempting to dominate criminals by using their own tools against them. What a different image is conjured by speaking of "healing addictions" rather than "fighting drugs"! Instead of "fighting" and "defeating" and "winning" we might attempt "healing" social ills, "negotiating with" our opponents, or "resolving" our problems.

Rather than using language of mastery, control, domination, opposition, or violent competition, we could use metaphors of birth, growth, creation, harmony, construction, transformation, journeying, healing, helping, loving, nurturing, cooperation and connection — all of which implant much healthier images in the unconscious mind.

Subtler-Yet-Powerful Aspects of Language

Man-Made Language

Power is always an issue in the way things are named and labeled. In the dominator cultures that shaped modern English, men controlled writing and printing and the "rules" of language. Therefore, men's perceptions and values are reflected in how things are named. Often, words associated with maleness have lofty, important meanings, while words associated with femaleness imply inferiority or pathology. For example, contrast "seminal" ideas with "hysterical" ideas; both adjectives come from the human reproductive system, but what a difference in meaning between the male and the female!

Another example: "master" (a person of great competency) and "mistress" (a man's illicit paramour).

The above examples of non-parallel terms reflect male power to name and define. So do gender-associated words that have no parallels for the other sex. Try to think of a female equivalent of "emasculated" or "virile." Or a parallel word for "feisty" or "dainty" that would apply to a man. What terms derived from female genitals are parallel in solemnity and importance to "testimony" or "testament" (derived from *testes*)?

Animal names are used to describe males and females in non-parallel ways. Those applied to women are often degrading or sexualized (heifer, filly, chick, dog, shrew, pig, sow, beaver, old crow, bunny, bitch, bat, fox, cold fish, hen, vixen, cat, kitten — usually paired with "sex") while those applied to men frequently reflect power, virility and cunning (buck, bull, stag, stallion, wolf). "Miss" and "Mrs." are traditional female "courtesy titles" that have no parallel male term. The title "Ms." has been adopted by many women since the 1970's as a parallel for "Mr." since neither "Mr." nor "Ms." provides information about an individual's marital status.

Language scholar Jackie Young writes: "It is our culture and communication system that constructs — and constricts — our reality, and if the male culture controls that system then our reality is created and shaped (constricted) by male perceptions" (1992, p. 98).

Seeing the Invisible and Creating the Nonexistent

In a partnership-oriented language, surely we would have more than one four-letter word ("love") to describe such varied forms of affection as romantic passion, long-standing friendship, the devotion of a long-married couple, the feeling of parent for child, the reverence of child for parent, the attachment of people and pets, enthusiasm for skiing, or a taste for vanilla ice cream!

What does it say about our culture that we have no single word for sexual intercourse that is neither clinical, violent, or taboo, yet we have so many different and graphic words to describe conflict and killing? Why are our most "obscene" oaths and expletives so often words for female sex organs or violent acts of dominator sex?

In addition to spoken and written language, it's important to pay attention to non-verbal communications — the "language" of behaviors such as eye contact, paying attention, changing the subject, interrupting, questioning, body movements, tone of voice, and "holding the floor" longest in conversation. In a partnership-ori-ented society, these behaviors would be evidenced fairly equally among women and men, and among people of different ages, races, or appearance. When they are not, it's likely that dominator dynamics are at work.

Transforming Language

How might we go about changing language to reflect a partnership orientation? Awareness, as discussed above, is a first step. Often it's possible to find less-common but still perfectly-serviceable words right in the English language. Using these words in place of commonly-used terms and expressions can create surprise in the listener, which in turn prompts them to listen more closely to the meaning of what we've actually *said*, and to contrast it with the meanings of the words we *didn't* say (but they expected).

If there isn't a readily-available alternative to androcentric or sexist or racist or ageist language, it's sometimes possible to playfully invent a word or expression whose meaning is perfectly clear and which calls attention to the problems inherent in the words *not* used. A woman might describe writing her last will and "ovariment." Or one might speak of finding a bunch of "senior singles" replacing "old maids." Such words, like "foremother" or "waitperson" may eventually find their way into general use; "Ms." has already done so. Although "prescriptive grammarians" (people whose goal is to define and enforce the rules of "proper" English) will be apoplectic about it, English is a living language, and we are perfectly free to make up new words, from "scratch" or by creative combining, as long as their meaning is clear.

To even speak of "partnership" itself — in a way that recognizes the centrality of the female/male relationship to all forms of social organization — requires the invention of new words. Riane Eisler coined the term "gylany"[1] to describe equal *linking* between men and women, rather than the hierarchical *ranking* of patriarchal domination. While "partnership" is used throughout this publication because of its familiarity to most people, it has the disadvantage of having many *other* meanings (business partnership, for example). "Gylany" is a more precise, but less-familiar term. Perhaps if it is used enough it will enter common usage, but in the meantime "partnership" gets the basic idea across, with less explanation. This is an example of the kind of trade-off that is often necessary in our efforts to change language and consciousness.

Speaking of Language

---

1. "Gy" comes from the Greek "gyne," or woman; "an" comes from "andros," or man. The "l" that links them comes from "lyein" or "lyo" which has double meanings in Greek: "to solve or resolve" (as in analysis) and "to dissolve or set free" (as in catalysis). From Eisler, Riane (1987). *The Chalice & the Blade: Our History, Our Future.* San Francisco: Harper & Rowe, p. 105.

The adjectives "sexist," "racist," "ageist," and "homophobic" are relatively recent inventions of the English language, created to describe attitudes of inequality which once were taken for granted as "natural." "Sexism" implies that one sex is better than the other, "racism" infers superior and inferior races, and so on. Language which is sexist, racist, ageist, and homophobic is often fairly obvious and easy to spot, once one understands the concepts.

But language can lack direct implications of inferiority, yet still promote inequality. It may be "androcentric" — treating male experience and perceptions as the norm while ignoring or trivializing female experience — without being overtly sexist. A quote from famous anthropologist Levi-Strauss is a perfect (if rather extreme) example of androcentrism: "All the people departed the next morning, leaving the women and children behind in the deserted village." Who are implicitly considered "people" in this statement, and who are not?

While religious language is not a major part of public school curriculum, in our private lives it's worth noting the androcentrism in "god-talk." With the exception of the growing "women's spirituality" movement and reform movements in several major monotheistic religions, traditional references to deity still use male terms. Some questions to consider: in a partnership-oriented culture, what would be considered sacred, and how would we discuss it? Would a supreme being be gendered at all, and would only one sex have a direct line to it, as in traditional religions?

Much of this chapter has focused on transforming language related to gender, for this reason: because the starting point of partnership is *gylany* (equal and interdependent relations between women and men),[2] the starting point for a language of partnership deals with the language of gender. But it does not stop there. Just as gylany implies equality, linking and cooperation in *all* human relationships, partnership language must describe equality, linking and cooperation among all groups of people, and between humans and all of nature, including the earth itself.

The Challenge of Change

In linguist Suzette Haden Elgin's visionary novel, *Native Tongue* (1984), women create their own language to express female perceptions and concerns which are not represented in their dominator culture's common language. It eventually causes completely unforeseen changes in consciousness, which affect every aspect of their lives. Trying to understand how this could have happened, one of the characters

---

2. The female/male relationship is a model for all other human relationships, not because it is more important than other forms, but because it is the one without which the species could not continue to exist.

plaintively asks: "How can you plan for a new reality when you don't have the remotest idea what it would be like?" The answer is, of course, that you can't — no science exists that can predict a new-paradigm world from within the old one.

So perhaps we can't completely predict what far-ranging effects a language of partnership might have on our individual consciousness or on our society. But we can see how the language and culture of domination and violence reinforce each other, and how continuing to speak in these terms can only bring us more of the same.

And we can ask: what might children be like who've learned to speak in terms of cooperation instead of competition, of creating and nurturing and healing instead of fighting and defeating and dominating? We can try presenting them with words and pictures (and experiences) of peace and pleasure and partnership, of art and music and dance, of love and sharing and caring — and we can watch what happens.

If we can even *begin* to imagine a world which respects and celebrates all life's diversity — and if we can educate our children with words and images and metaphors that describe this vision, perhaps our children will be the ones to bring our vision to life!

Some Common Words and Phrases and their Partnership Alternatives	
Dominator	Alternative
Consciousness-*raising*	Consciousness-*expansion*
Deadline or *Target date*	*Goal*
Dear Sir or *Madam*	*Greetings*
Fellow man	*Human kin*
Fight crime	*Eliminate* crime
Fight injustice	*Heal* injustice
Man the office	*Staff* the office
Mankind	*Humankind*
Miss or *Mrs.*	*Ms.*
Opposite sex	*Other* sex
No-man's land	*No-one's* land
Rule of thumb	*Guideline*
Spearhead an effort	*Initiate* an effort
War of the sexes	*Dance of the sexes*
Win-win solution	*Grow-grow* solution
You *guys* (for both men and women)	You *gaias* (for both)
Kill two birds with one stone	*Hatch two birds from one egg* or *Feed two birds with one hand*

Riane Eisler
Selected References

Books

The chalice and the blade: Our history, our future, San Francisco: Harper & Row, 1987, 1988. Published in Japanese by Hosei University Press (Tokyo), in French by Laffont (Paris), in German by Bertelsmann Verlag and Goldmann Verlag (Munich), in Finnish by Werner Soderstrom Osakeyhtio (Helsinki), in Italian by Pratiche Editrice (Milan), in Portuguese by Imago (Rio de Janeiro, Brazil) and by Via Optima (Portugual), in Spanish by Editorial Cuatro Vientos (Santiago de Chile), in Great Britain and Australia by Harper Collins (London), in Greek by Glaros (Athens), in Danish by Gyldendalske Boghandel (Copenhagen), in Norwegian by Pax (Oslo), in Russian by Ecopolis Foundation (Moscow), in Dutch by Entheon (Nijmegen), in Chinese by Chinese Academy of Social Sciences (Beijing), and in Czech by Nakladatelstvi Lidove Noviny (Prague).

The chalice and the blade audio cassette. 1997. Novato, California: New World Library.

Sacred pleasure: Sex, myth, and the politics of the body, San Francisco: Harper Collins, 1995, 1996. To date, foreign rights have been acquired by Hosei University Press (Tokyo), Element/Penguin (London), Transworld Publishers/Bantam (Moorebank, South Wales, Australia), Edizioni Frassinelli (Milan), Editorial Cuatro Vientos (Santiago de Chile), and Rocco (Rio de Janeiro).

With David Loye, and Kari Norgaard. 1995. *Women, men, and the global quality of life*, Pacific Grove, CA: Center for Partnership Studies.

Tomorrow's children: Education for the 21st century. Contact Center for Partnership Studies or check CPS website <www.partnershipway.org> for publication information.

Learning for living: Fifteen partnership literacies and competencies. In preparation. Contact Center for Partnership Studies or check CPS website rtnershipway.org for publication information.

With Allie C. Hixson. 1986. *The ERA facts and action guide*. Washington, DC: National Women's Conference Committee.

The equal rights handbook: What ERA means to your life, your rights, and the future. 1978. New York: Avon.

Dissolution: No-fault divorce, marriage, and the future of women. 1977. New York: McGraw-Hill.

Chapters in Books

Cultural transformation theory: A new paradigm for history. 1997. In *Macrohistory and macrohistorians*, edited by Johan Galtung and Sohail Inayatullah. Westport, CT: Praeger.

From domination to partnership: The hidden subtext for sustainable change. 1997. In *The new business of business*, edited by Maya Porter. San Francisco: Berrett-Koehler.

Human rights and violence: Integrating the private and public spheres. 1996. In *The web of violence*, edited by Lester Kurtz and Jennifer Turpin.Urbana, IL: University of Illinois Press.

Foundations for a new world order. 1993. In *The new paradigm in business: Emerging strategies for leadership and organizational change*, edited by Michael Ray and Alan Renzler. Los Angeles: Tarcher.

The long journey home. 1990. In *For the love of God: New writings by spiritual and psychological leaders*, edited by Benjamin Shield and Richard Carlson. San Rafael, CA: New World Library.

The Gaia tradition and the partnership future. 1990. In *Reweaving the world: The emergence of ecofeminism*, edited by Irene Diamond and Gloria Orenstein. San Francisco: Sierra Club Books.

Eisler, Riane, and David Loye. 1986. Population pressure, women's roles, and peace. In *World encyclopedia of peace*, edited by Ervin Laszlo and Yong-youl Yoo. London: Pergamon.

Eisler, Riane, and David Loye. 1986. Peace and feminist thought: New directions. In *World encyclopedia of peace*, edited by Ervin Laszlo and Yong-youl Yoo. London: Pergamon.

Loye, David, and Riane Eisler. 1986. The relation of sexual equality to peace. In *World encyclopedia of peace*, edited by Ervin Laszlo and Yong-youl Yoo. London: Pergamon.

Books (Interviews)

Hanlon, Gail, ed. 1997. *Voicing power: Conversations with visionary women*. New York: HarperCollins.

Callahan, Matthew.1993. *Sex, death, & the angry young man: Conversations with Riane Eisler and David Loye*. Ojai, California: Times Change Press.

Articles

Changing the rules of the game: Work, values, and our future. 1998. Pacific Grove, California: Center for Partnership Studies. Available from the Center for Partnership Studies or the CPS website <www.partnershipway.org.>

A partnership world. 1995. *UNESCO Courier* for the 1995 United Nations Women's Conference (September).

From domination to partnership: The hidden subtext for sustainable change. 1994. *Journal of Organizational Change Management* 7(4). Different versions of this article have also been published in *World Business Academy Perspectives* 9(3), 1995, and *Training and Development Journal* 49(2), 1995.

Women, men, and management: Redesigning our future. 1991. *Futures* 23(1).

The partnership society. 1989. *Futures* 21(1, February).

Technology at the turning point. 1988. *Woman of Power* 11 (fall).

Human rights: Toward an integrated theory for action. 1987. *Feminist Issues* 7(1, spring) and *The Human Rights Quarterly* 9(3) August 1987. Also published in *Nordic Journal on Human Rights*, August 5, 1987 and in *Foreign Social Sciences*, (a publication of the Chinese Academy of Social Sciences), Oct 1989, and read into the U.S. *Congressional Record* by Senator Allan Cranston.

Eisler, Riane, and David Loye. 1985. Will women change the world? A report on the U.N. End of the Decade for Women Conference, Nairobi, 19 85. *Futures* 17(5): 550-554.

Nairobi 1985: A window of hope. 1985. *The Humanist* 45(6): 21-23 (November/December).

Eisler, Riane, and David Loye. 1983. The failure of liberalism: A reassessment of ideology from a new feminine-masculine perspective. *Political Psychology* 4(2): 375-391.

Eisler, Riane, and David Loye. 1980. Childhood and the chosen future. *Journal of Clinical Child Psychology* 9(2): 102-106 (summer).

David Loye
Selected References

The Healing of a Nation. 1972. New York: Delta.

Loye, D., and M. Rokeach. 1976. Ideology, belief systems, values, and attitudes. In *International encyclopedia of neurology, psychiatry, psychoanalysis and psychology*. New York: Van Nostrand.

Loye, D., R. Gorney, and G. Steele. 1977. Effects of television: An experimental field study. *Journal of Communications* 27(3): 206-216.

The leadership passion: A psychology of ideology. 1977. San Francisco: Jossey-Bass.

The Knowable Future: A Psychology of Forecasting and Prophecy. 1978. Wiley-Interscience.

Television effects: It's not all bad news. 1978. *Psychology Today* (May).

Ideology and prediction. 1980. *Technological Forecasting and Social Change* 16: 229-242.

Personality and prediction. 1980. *Technological Forecasting and Social Change* 16: 93-104.

The Sphinx and the rainbow: Brain, mind and future vision. 1983. Boston: Shambhala.

The brain, the mind, and the future. 1983. *Technological Forecasting and Social Change* 23: 267-280.

Gehirn, Geist und Vision: Das Potential unseres Bewusstseins die Zukunft vorauszusehen und zu gestalten. 1985. Basel, Switzerland: Sphinx Verlag.

Japanese edition of *The Sphinx and the rainbow*. 1985. Tokyo: Saido Sha.

The lonesome and the not so lonesome strangers: Men at the Nairobi conference. 1985. *The Humanist* 45(6).

Moral development and peace. 1986. In *World Encyclopedia of Peace*, edited by E. Laszlo and Y. Yoo. London: Pergamon.

Loye, D., and R. Eisler. 1986. Sexual equality and peace. In *World Encyclopedia of Peace*, edited by E. Laszlo and Y. Yoo. London: Pergamon.

De sfinx en de regenboog: Hersenen, geest en toekomstvisie. 1986. Den Haag, Netherlands: Mirananda.

Loye, D., and R. Eisler, R. 1987. Chaos and transformation: The implications of natural scientific nonequilibrium theory for social science and society. *Behavioral Science* 32(1): 53-65.

La mente umana e l'immagine del futuro. 1988. In *Physis: Abitare La Terra*, edited by M. Ceruti and E. Laszlo. Milan, Italy: Feltrinelli.

Hemisphericity and creativity: Group process and the dream factory. 1988. In *Hemispheric specialization, affect and creativity*, edited by K. Hoppe. Psychiatric Clinics of North America.

The partnership society: Personal practice. 1989. *Futures* (February).

Moral sensitivity and the evolution of higher mind. 1990. *World Futures: The Journal of General Evolution* 30: 41-52.

Chaos and transformation: Implications of non-equilibrium theory for social science and society. 1990. In *The New Evolutionary Paradigm*, edited by E. Laszlo. New York: Gordon and Breach.

Cooperation and moral sensitivity. 1992. In *Cooperation: Beyond the age of competition*, edited by Allan Combs. Philadelphia: Gordon and Breach.

Moral sensitivity and the evolution of higher mind. 1993. In *The evolution of cognitive maps: New paradigms for the twenty-first century*, edited by Ervin Laszlo, Ignazio Masuli, Robert Artigiani, and Vilmos Csanyi. Philadelphia: Gordon and Breach.

Charles Darwin, Paul MacLean, and the lost origins of "the moral sense": Some implications for general evolution theory. 1994. *World Futures: The Journal of General Evolution* 40: 187-196.

Prediction in chaotic social, economic, and political conditions: The conflict between traditional chaos theory and the psychology of prediction, and some implications for general evolution theory. 1995. *World Futures: The Journal of General Evolution* 44: 15-31.

How predictable is the future: The conflict between traditional chaos theory and the psychology of prediction, and the challenge for chaos psychology. 1995. In *Chaos theory in psychology and the life sciences*, edited by Robin Robertson and Allan Combs. Mahwah, NJ: Erlebaum.

La psichiatria di Gilania: Moralita del dominio and moralita della partnership. (The psychiatric consequences of androcratic and gylanic morality). 1996. *Pluriverso* 1(3): 11-118.

Frank and I and the research that wasn't: Or why the streets run red with blood on TV and in the real world. 1996. In *Unusual associates: A Festschrift for Frank Barron*, edited by Alfonso Montuori. Cresskill, NJ: Hampton Press.

Scientific foundations for a global ethic at a time of evolutionary crisis. In The dialectic of evolution: Essays in honor of David Loye, edited by A. Montuori. 1997. *World Future: The Journal of General Evolution* 49(1-2): 3-17.

Loye, D., ed. 1998. *The evolutionary outrider: The impact of the human agent on evolution.* Westport, CT: Praeger.

A brief outline of evolutionary action theory. 1998. In *The evolutionary outrider*, edited by D. Loye.

A brief history of the general evolution research group. 1998. In *The evolutionary outrider*, edited by D. Loye.

Darwin's lost theory: A vision for the 21st century. (book in preparation).

Darwin's lost heirs: In pursuit of the vision, the greater theory, and the better future. (book in preparation).

General References

Abbott, Edwin. 1952. *Flatland*. New York: Dover.

Aburdene, Patricia, and John Naisbitt. 1992. *Megatrends for women*. New York: Villard.

Adorno, T. W., Else Frenkel-Brunswick, Daniel Levinson, and R. Nevitt Stanford. 1964. *The authoritarian personality*. New York: Wiley.

Aristophanes. 1987. *Lysistrata*. Edited by Jeffrey Henderson. Oxford University Press.

Barry, Kathleen. 1979. *Female sexual slavery*. New York: Avon.

Barstow, Anne Llewellyn. 1994. *Witchcraze: A new history of the European witch hunts*. London and San Francisco: Pandora.

Beard, Mary. 1946. *Woman as a force in history*. New York: Macmillan.

Beneke, Tim. 1993. Deep masculinity as social control: Foucault, Bly and masculinity. *Masculinities* 1 (summer): 13-19.

Berry, David S. 1993. Growing up violent. *Media and Values* (summer).

Boulding, Elise. 1976. *The underside of history: A view of women through time*. Boulder, CO: Westview Press.

Bradshaw, John. 1988. *Bradshaw on the family*. Pompano Beach, FL: Health Communications.

Brod, Harry. 1987. *The making of masculinities*. Boston: Allen & Unwin.

Brown, Lester R. 1995. *State of the world 1995: A Worldwatch Institute report on progress toward a sustainable society*. New York: Norton.

Caldicott, Helen. *Nuclear Madness*. New York: Bantam, 1980.

Callahan, Mathew. 1993. *Sex, death, and the angry young man: Conversations with Riane Eisler and David Loye*. Ojai, CA: Times Change Press.

Capra, Fritjof. 1982. *The turning point*. New York: Simon & Schuster.

Carson, Rachel. 1962. *Silent spring*. Boston: Houghton Mifflin, 1962.

Chamberlin, Roy B., and Herman Feldman, eds. 1950. *The Dartmouth Bible*. Boston: Houghton Mifflin.

Christ, Carol P., and Judith Plaskow, eds. 1979. *Womanspirit rising*. San Francisco: Harper & Row.

Coltrane, Scott. 1988. Father-child relationships and the status of women." *American Journal of Sociology*, 93 (March).

Conner, Randy P. 1993. *Blossom of bone: Reclaiming the connections between homoeroticism and the sacred*. San Francisco: HarperCollins.

Daly, Mary. 1978. *Gyn/ecology: The metaethics of radical feminism.* Boston: Beacon Press.

De Waal, Frans. 1989. *Peacemaking among primates.* Cambridge, MA: Oxford University Press.

Elgin, Suzette Haden. 1984. *Native tongue.* New York: Daw Books.

Evershed, Jane. 1994. *More than a tea party.* San Francisco: HarperSanFrancisco.

Fausto-Sterling, Anne. 1984. *Myths of gender: Biological theories about women and men.* 2d ed. New York: Pergamon.

Fedigan, Linda Marie. 1982. *Primate paradigms: Sex roles and social bonds.* Montreal: Eden Press.

Ferguson, Marilyn. 1980. *The aquarian conspiracy: Personal and social transformation in the 1980s.* Los Angeles: Tarcher.

Fiorenza, Elisabeth Schüssler. 1983. *In memory of her.* New York: Crossroad.

Fisher, Roger, and William Ury. 1981. *Getting to yes: Negotiating agreement without giving in.* Boston: Houghton Mifflin.

Fisher, Roger, and Scott Brown. 1988. *Getting together: Building relationships.* Boston: Houghton Mifflin.

Fletcher, Ronald. 1970. The making of the modern family. In *The family and its future,* edited by Katherine Elliott. London: Churchill.

Fromm, Erich. 1941. *Escape from freedom.* New York: Holt, Rinehart & Winston.

Gablik, Suzi. 1991. *The reenchantment of art.* New York: Thames and Hudson.

Galtung, Johan, and Sohail Inayatullah, eds. 1997. *Macrohistory and macrohistorians: Perspectives on individual, social and civilizational change.* New York: Praeger.

Gerbner, George. 1993. Women and minorities in television: A study in casting and fate. In *Report to the Screen Actors Guild and the American Federation of Radio and Television Artists* (June).

Gerbner, George. 1995. Marketing Global Mayhem. *The Public* 2(2).

Gerbner, George, Larry Gross, Michael Morgan, and Nancy Signorielli. 1994. Growing up with television: The cultivation perspective. In *Media effects: Advances in theory and research,* edited by Bryant Jennings and Dolf Zillmann. Hillsdale, N.J.: Erlbaum.

Gerzon, Mark. 1982. *A choice of heroes: The changing face of American manhood.* Boston: Houghton Mifflin.

Gilligan, Carol. 1982. *In a different voice.* Boston: Harvard University Press.

Gilman, Charlotte Perkins. 1979. *Herland.* New York: Pantheon.

Gimbutas, Marija. 1980. *The early civilization of Europe.* Monograph for Indo-European Studies 131, University of California at Los Angeles.

Gimbutas, Marija. 1982. *The goddesses and gods of old Europe.* Berkeley: University of California Press.

Gimbutas, Marija. 1989. *The language of the goddess.* San Francisco: Harper & Row.

Gimbutas, Marija. 1991. *The civilization of the goddess.* San Francisco: HarperSanFrancisco.

Gray, Elizabeth Dodson, ed. 1988. *Sacred dimensions of women's experience.* Wellesley, MA: Roundtable Press.

Gross, Bertram. 1980. *Friendly fascism: The new face of power in America.* Boston: South End Press.

Hagen, Kay Leigh, ed. 1992. *Women respond to the men's movement.* San Francisco: Harper.

Harman, Willis. 1988. *Global mind change.* Indianapolis: Knowledge Systems.

Hawkes, Jacquetta. 1968. *The dawn of the gods: Minoan and Mycenaean origins of Greece.* New York: Random House.

Heilbroner, Robert. 1961. *The worldly philosophers.* New York: Simon & Schuster.

Henderson, Hazel. 1981. *The politics of the solar age: Alternatives to economics.* New York: Anchor Books.

hooks, bell. 1984. *Feminist theory: From margin to center.* Boston: South End Press.

Hussey, Edward. 1972. *The Pre-Socratics.* New York: Scribner's.

Huston, Perdita. 1979. *Third world women speak out.* New York: Praeger.

Iglehart, Hallie Austin. 1983. *Womanspirit.* San Francisco: Harper & Row.

Jaln, Devaki, and Nirmala Bannerjee, eds. 1985. *Women in poverty: Tyranny of the household.* New Delhi: Shakti Books.

Jiayin, Min, ed. 1995. *The Chalice and the Blade in Chinese Culture.* Beijing: China Social Sciences Publishing House.

Johnson, Sonia. 1983. *From Housewife to Heretic.* New York: Anchor.

Keller, Mara L. 1988. The Eleusinian mysteries of Demeter and Persephone: Fertility, sexuality, and rebirth. *Journal of Feminist Studies in Religion* 4 (Spring).

Kerber, Linda, and Jane DeHart Mathews, eds. 1982. *Women's America.* New York: Oxford University Press.

Keuls, Eva. 1993. *The Reign of the phallus: Sexual politics in ancient Athens.* Berkeley: University of California Press.

Kiefer, Charles F., and Peter M. Senge. 1982. *Metanoic organizations: Experiments in organizational innovation.* Innovation Associates.

Kimmel, Michael S., and Thomas E. Mosmiller, eds. 1992. *Against the tide: Pro-feminist men in the United States 1776-1990.* Boston: Beacon Press.

Kivel, Paul. 1992. *Men's work: How to stop the violence that tears our lives apart.* New York: Ballantine.

Koegel, Rob. 1994. Healing the wounds of masculinity: A crucial role for educators. *Holistic Education Review* 7 (March).

Kramer, Samuel Noah, and John Maier. 1989. *Myths of Enki, the crafty god.* New York: Oxford University Press.

Kurtz, Ron. 1988. *Hakomi therapy.* Ashland, OR: Hakomi of Ashland.

Kohn, Alfie. 1987. *No contest: The case against competition.* Boston: Houghton Mifflin.

Laszlo, Ervin. 1987. *Evolution: The grand synthesis.* Boston: Shambhala.

Lebell, Sharon. 1988. *Naming ourselves, Naming our children: Resolving the last name dilemma.* Freedom, CA: Crossing Press.

Lewontin, R. C., Steven Rose, and Leon J. Kamin. 1984. *Not in our genes.* New York: Pantheon.

Lorde, Audre. 1984. Uses of the erotic: The erotic as power. In *Sister outsider, Essays and speeches by Audre Lorde.* Freedom, CA: Crossing Press.

Luce, J. V. 1969. *The end of Atlantis.* London: Thames & Hudson.

Marshack, Alexander. 1972. *The roots of civilization.* New York: McGraw-Hill.

Marx, Karl, and Friedrich Engels. 1978. The communist manifesto. In *The Marx-Engels reader,* edited by Robert Tucker. New York: Norton.

McHale, John. 1969. *The future of the future.* New York: Ballantine.

Mellaart, James. 1967. *Catal Huyuk.* New York: McGraw-Hill.

Miller, Alice. 1983. *For your own good: Hidden cruelty in child-rearing and the roots of violence.* New York: Farrar, Straus, Giroux.

Miller, Jean Baker. 1986. *Toward a new psychology of women,* 2d ed. Boston: Beacon.

Miller, Casey, and Kate Swift, eds. 1977. *Words and women.* New York: Anchor.

Millett, Kate. 1970. *Sexual politics.* New York: Doubleday.

Mollenkott, Virginia. 1988. *Women, men, and the Bible.* New York: Crossroad.

Montagu, Ashley. 1976. *The nature of human aggression.* New York: Oxford University Press.

Montuori, Alfonso, and Isabella Conti. 1993. *From power to partnership.* San Francisco: HarperCollins.

Morgan, Robin, ed. 1984. *Sisterhood is global: The first anthology of writings from the international women's movement.* New York: Anchor-Doubleday.

Neumann, Erich. 1955. *The great mother.* Princeton, NJ: Princeton University Press.

Noble, David F. 1992. *A world without women: The Christian clerical culture of Western science.* New York: Knopf.

Noble, Vicki. 1983. *Motherpeace: A way to the goddess through myth, art, and tarot.* San Francisco: Harper & Row.

Noddings, Nel. 1992.*The challenge to care in schools.* New York: Teachers College Press.

Noddings, Nel. 1994. Learning to engage in moral dialogue. *Holistic Education Review* 7(2).

Okin, Susan Moller. 1979. *Women in Western political thought.* Princeton, NJ: Princeton University Press.

Orenstein, Gloria. 1990. *The reflowering of the goddess.* New York: Pergamon.

Orwell, George. 1949. *1984*. New York: Harcourt Brace.

Pagels, Elaine. 1979. *The gnostic gospels*. New York: Random House.

Patai, Raphael. 1978. *The Hebrew goddess*. New York: Arno.

Pietilä, Hilkka, and Jeanne Vickers. 1994. *Making women matter: The role of the United Nations*. London: Zed Books.

Plaskow, Judith. 1990. *Standing again at Sinai: Judaism from a feminine perspective*. New York: Harper & Row.

Plato. 1945. *The Republic*. Translated by Francis MacDonald Coonford. New York: Oxford University Press.

Platon, Nikolas. 1966. *Crete*. Archeologia Mundi Series. Geneva: Nagel.

Ranck, Shirley Ann. 1986. *Cakes for the queen of heaven*. Boston: Unitarian Universalist Association.

Reardon, Betty. 1985. *Sexism and the war system*. New York: Teachers College Press.

Rich, Adrienne. 1977. *Of woman born*. New York: Bantam.

Rich, Adrienne. 1985. *The fact of a doorframe*. New York: Norton.

Ricci, Isolina. 1980. *Mom's house, Dad's house: Making shared custody work*. New York: Macmillan.

Robbins, John. 1996. *Reclaiming our health*. Tiburon, California: Kramer.

Robinson, John Mansley. 1968. *An introduction to early Greek philosophers*. Boston: Houghton Mifflin.

Rockwell, Joan. 1974. *Fact in fiction: The use of literature in the systematic study of society*. London: Routledge & Kegan Paul.

Roszak, Betty, and Theodore Roszak. 1969. The hard and the soft. In *Masculine/Feminine*, edited by Betty Roszak and Theodore Roszak. New York: Harper Colophon.

Ruether, Rosemary Radford, ed. 1974. *Religion and sexism*. New York: Touchstone.

Sahtouris, Elisabeth. 1989. *Gaia: The human journey from chaos to cosmos*. New York: Pocket Books.

Salk, Jonas. 1983. *Anatomy of reality*. New York: Columbia University Press.

Sappho. 1965. *Lyrics in the original Greek*. Translated by Wilis Barnstone. New York: Anchor.

Schaef, Anne Wilson. 1987. *When society becomes an addict*. San Francisco: Harper & Row.

Schneir, Miriam, ed. 1994. *Feminism in our time*. New York: Vintage.

Schneir, Miriam, ed. 1972. *Feminism: The essential historical writings*. New York: Vintage.

Sen, Gita. 1985. *Development, crisis, and alternative visions: Third world women's perspectives*. New Delhi, India: DAWN Secretariat.

Signell, Karen. 1990. *Wisdom of the heart: Working with women's dreams*. New York: Bantam.

Sivard, Ruth. 1983. *World military and social expenditures.* Washington: World Priorities.

Sleeter, Christine E. 1996. *Multicultural education as social activism.* Albany, New York: SUNY Press.

Sleeter, Christine E., and Carl A. Grant, eds. 1994. *Making choices for multicultural education.* Columbus, Ohio: Merrill.

Spender, Dale, ed. 1983. *Feminist theorists: Three centuries of key women thinkers.* New York: Pantheon.

Spretnak, Charlene, and Fritjof Capra. 1986. *Green politics: The global promise.* Santa Fe, NM: Bear.

Stanton, Elizabeth Cady. 1974. The woman's Bible. Reprinted in *The original feminist attack on the Bible.* New York: Arno.

Starhawk. 1979. *The spiral dance: Rebirth of the ancient religion of the goddess.* San Francisco: Harper & Row.

Steinem, Gloria. 1983. *Outrageous acts and everyday rebellions.* New York: Holt, Reinhart & Winston.

Stoltenberg, John. 1990. *Refusing to be a man: Essays on sex and justice.* New York: Meridian.

Stone, Merlin. 1976. *When God was a woman.* New York: Harvest.

Tanner, Nancy. 1981. *On becoming human.* Boston: Cambridge University Press.

Taylor, G. Rattray. 1954. *Sex in history.* New York: Ballantine.

Theobald, Robert. 1987. *The rapids of change: Social entrepreneurship in turbulent times.* Indianapolis, IN: Knowledge Systems.

Tobach, Ethel, and Betty Rosof, eds. 1978. *Genes and gender.* New York: Gordian.

Utain, Marsha. 1989. *Stepping out of chaos.* Deerfield Beach, FL: Health Communications.

Waring, Marilyn. 1988. *If women counted: A new feminist economics.* San Francisco: Harper & Row.

Wehr, Demaris. 1987. *Jung and feminism.* Boston: Beacon.

Weinhold, Barry K., and Janae B. Weinhold. 1989. *Breaking free of the co-dependency trap.* Walpole, NH: Stillpoint.

West, Cornel. 1993. *Race matters.* Boston: Beacon.

Wilshire, Donna. 1994. *Virgin, mother, crone: Myths and mysteries of the triple goddess.* Rochester, VT: Inner Traditions.

Wittig, Monique. 1985. *Les guerilleres.* Translated by David Le Vey. Boston: Beacon.

Wolf, Linda, and K. Wind Hughes. 1997. *Daughters of the moon, sisters of the sun: Young women and mentors on the transition to womanhood.* Stonybrook, CT: New Society.

Women's International News Network (WIN) News, Fran Hosken, publisher, 187 Grant Street, Lexington, MA 02173-2140.

Young, Jacqueline. 1992. Unpublished doctoral dissertation. The Union Institute.

Zihlman, Adrienne. 1997. Women's bodies, women's lives: An evolutionary perspective. In *The evolving female: A life-history perspective*, edited by Mary Ellen Morbeck, Alison Galloway, and Adrienne L. Zihlman. Princeton, N.J.: Princeton University Press.

Resources for
Group Organizers

LOVE, JOY, AND THE GRACE, BEAUTY, AND WONDER OF LIFE ARE CAPTURED IN
THESE ANCIENT PARTNERS — TWO BIRDS FROM THE FAMOUS SPRING FRESCO WITH
ITS EXTRAVAGANT VEGETATION UNCOVERED IN THE EXCAVATION OF THE
MINOAN SETTLEMENT ON THE ISLAND OF THERA NEAR CRETE. IT WAS PAINTED
ABOUT 1500 B.C.

About
The Chalice and the Blade

Hailed by Princeton anthropologist Ashley Montagu as "the most important book since Darwin's *Origin of Species*," *The Chalice and the Blade* has not only had a remarkable publishing history, it has also launched a global movement.

Since its original publication by Harper & Row in 1987, it has been translated into 16 languages and went into its *25th* printing in 1995 with a new epilogue. In addition to its profound impact on the thousands of women and men who report that it has changed their lives, *The Chalice and the Blade* influences the arts, music, politics, business, academia, the healing professions, literature, and the media.

The Chalice and the Blade also:

- led to the formation of the Center for Partnership Studies, dedicated to turning the book's ideas into action,

- united women and men from around the world, leading to the formation of the International Partnership Network,

- prompted a group of prominent Chinese scholars at the Chinese Academy of Social Sciences in Beijing to form the Chinese Partnership Research Group, whose groundbreaking analysis of China's past and present was published in 1995, entitled *The Chalice and the Blade in Chinese Culture*,

- was the foundation for the First International Partnership Conference, held on the Mediterranean island of Crete and attended by 500 people from more than 40 nations,

- has inspired the spontaneous formation of study groups worldwide,

- has been adopted as a text in courses on peace studies, philosophy, sociology, Western history, women's studies, and other disciplines in the humanities and social sciences,

- has led to the development of Partnership Studies courses at Prescott College and the California Institute for Integral Studies,

- has been widely used by therapists who are recommending it to patients and find it catalytic for healing, and by business people who have successfully applied its ideas to their companies,

- has influenced more than 100 books, including Patricia Aburden's and John Naisbitt's bestselling *Megatrends for Women,* Suzi Gablik's *The Reenchantment of Art,* Samuel Noah Kramer's and John Maier's *The Myths of Enki,* Andreas Giger's *Eine Welt für Alle,* Gianlucca Bocchi's and Mauro Ceruti's *Origini di Storie,* and Alfonso Montuori's and Isabella Conti's *From Power to Partnership.*

The following is a selection of quotes that provides a good, quick sense of the book and its significance. A review by Helen Knode that originally apeared in *L.A. Weekly* follows in the next section.

"Apart from Darwin's *Origin of Species,* no book has impressed me as profoundly as *The Chalice and the Blade.*" (Ashley Montagu, Princeton anthropologist)

"Everyone.. .should have the opportunity to read it." (*Chicago Tribune*)

"...fascinating reading." (*Booklist*)

"The greatest murder mystery and cover-up of all time." (*New Age Journal*)

"...a blueprint for a better future. ..validates a belief in humanity's capacity for benevolence and cooperation." (*San Francisco Chronicle*)

"...clears up many historical mysteries.. .provides foundations upon which to build a more humanistic world." (*The Humanist*)

"...one of the most important books of the year." (*Minneapolis Star & Tribune*)

"...an imaginative and persuasive work." (*Library Journal*)

"...an ambitious new synthesis.. .rigorous research. ..traces the unseen forces that shape human culture." (*Los Angeles Times*)

"...casts new light on all major problems.. .brings new clarity to the entire man-woman question... a major contribution." (Jean Baker Miller, M.D., director Stone Center, Wellesley College)

"...both scholarly and passionate. ..essential reading." (Fritjof Capra, physicist)

"Some books are revelations, they open the spirit to the unimaginable possibilities. *The Chalice and the Blade* is one of those magnificient key books..." (Isabel Allende, author of *The House of the Spirits*)

"...perhaps a key to our survival. ..an enormous achievement." (Daniel Ellsberg, former Pentagon advisor)

"...a daring journey from pole to pole of human existence." (Charles Tilly, professor of history, New School for Social Research)

"A gem … a rare combination of poetic expression and sober substance." (Jessie Bernard, professor of sociology)

"...a notable application of science to the growth and survival of human understanding." (Maria Gimbutas, professor of archeology, UCLA)

"...shows how our political and economic systems may attain a new balance." (Hazel Henderson, futurist)

"...a very important picture of human evolution." (Nikolas Platon, former director, Acropolis Museum, Athens)

"...required reading for anyone who is concerned about our destiny on Earth." (Ervin Laszlo, former director of research, United Nations)

"...an exciting and germinal work." (Robert Jungk, winner 1986 Alternative Nobel Peace Prize)

"...a catalytic and pioneering example of general evolution theory at work." (Ralph Abraham, professor, UCSC)

"A groundbreaking book...brilliant research...will greatly influence and change our lives." (*Women's International Network News*)

"...as important, perhaps more important, than the unearthing of Troy or the deciphering of cuneiform." (Bruce Wilshire, professor of philosophy, Rutgers University)

Apocalypse No

A Review of
The Chalice and the Blade

Helen Knode

The Chalice and the Blade may be the most significant work published in all our lifetimes. Princeton anthropologist Ashley Montagu calls it "the most important book since Darwin's *Origin of Species.*" Start reading it; it doesn't appear to be earth-shattering. Futurist/feminist/international legal expert Riane Eisler has a very unhurried, straightforward manner of communicating her thoughts. No portentousness, no scary visions of hell, no big claims about her mission to save humankind. Yet motivating *The Chalice and the Blade* are some profoundly radical questions:

"Why do we hunt and persecute each other?" Eisler asks in the introduction to her book. "Why is our world so full of man's infamous inhumanity to man—and to woman? How can human beings be so brutal to their own kind? What is it that chronically tilts us toward cruelty rather than kindness, toward war rather than peace, toward destruction rather then actualization?"

In these four innocent-seeming questions, Eisler challenges a whole range of deeply ingrained assumptions: that human beings are each other's mortal enemies, that competitiveness between people is natural, and that the biological difference between men and women dictates women's subordinate status. (In other words, she's challenging the social-scientist/philosopher she's compared to, Darwin.) She's also ultimately asking the question: Do we have to destroy our species and the planet in a nuclear war?

Eisler's answers are as radical, and as radically simple, as her questions: No, humans don't have to hate and oppress each other. No, women are not naturally inferior to men. No, deadly competitiveness is not intrinsic to human nature. And no,

Excerpts of a review originally published in the *L.A. Weekly*, June 19-25, 1987.

we don't have to die in a great ball of fire. In the end, *The Chalice and the Blade* offers hope.

If Eisler presented no evidence for her claims, however comforting they might be, she'd just be another run-of-the-mill utopian, a dreamy New Ager on the loose. But she has mustered, organized, and interpreted a staggering amount of proof that for 15,000 years of human history, people lived in relative peace, women were not an underclass, and society was not rigidly stratified with the rich at the top, the poor at the bottom. In addition, contrary to the notion that only competition produces human progress, Eisler shows how the societies of the Neolithic age (from approximately 6000 B.C.E.) developed all the basic tools and technologies that we use today—agriculture, metallurgy, architecture, urban planning, writing, weaving, sanitation. These peoples also worshiped not a cruel God or an array of capricious, vengeful gods, but the Great Goddess, symbol of fertility, life, regeneration, and the bounty of the earth.

Eisler traces the evolution of these ancient cultures—as well as she can, given the incompleteness of the record—aided by the work of a variety of archeologists. She notes what we already knew: that beginning somewhere around 4000 B.C.E. successive waves of barbarians swept into the European and Middle Eastern areas surrounding the Mediterranean and destroyed many Bronze Age civilizations, the most important being the Minoan on Crete. By approximately 2500 B.C.E., the ancient world had been utterly changed—derailed, Eisler would say. Slavery, war, fortified cities, the male rule of force, religions of fear, the use of technology for destructive purposes—all of these things had been introduced into formerly harmonious, Goddess-worshiping, highly evolved cultures.

Eisler proposes two models, *partnership* and *dominator*, exquisite in their clarity, that describe two fundamentally different ways of organizing human society. The originality of her paradigm comes from the fact that she wants to include women's history in the study of human history, which, in practice, means the history of men. Eisler believes that the way the relations between men and women are structured "has a profound effect on every one of our institutions, on our values, and on the direction of our cultural evolution, particularly whether it will be peaceful or warlike."

For many millennia, communities were organized along partnership lines. People were "linked," not "ranked," in Eisler's terms. Women were respected as life-givers and priestesses, but they did not run the show: These societies were sexually egalitarian. (Eisler makes it very clear that the alternative to patriarchy is not necessarily matriarchy.) Hierarchies of dominance, on the other hand, maintained by force or the threat of force, were brought from the peripheries of the civilized world by the barbarians, here called Kurgans. It took several thousand years, but strongman rule was finally established, inaugurating what Eisler terms "a 5,000-year dominator detour." This detour quite literally turned the direction of our cultural evolution around, and it continues to determine the world as we know it today.

Not completely, of course. Neither of these systems is monolithic. The partnership societies were not structureless, leaderless, horizontally linked societies; the dominator model does not entail an absolutely pyramidal society perpetuated by, and perpetuating, violence against people and nature. In fact, Eisler postulates that the course of history is shaped by the tensions between these two alternative systems. At some points, such as around the time of Jesus and in the Renaissance, the partnership drive is in the ascendant. At other, more frequent points, the dominator model is strongest: We're living in one of those periods now. Eisler believes that the stronger the push toward a more egalitarian, peaceful, ecologically sound society, the more strenuously the forces opposed to all that (the dominator or "androcratic" forces) reassert themselves. In the 1980s there were very strong movements for peace and social justice, for instance, and that triggered the repressive responses in Christian fundamentalist circles and among right-wingers in the government.

While this simple formulation represents ten years of work, it isn't the most difficult aspect of *The Chalice and the Blade's* argument. The most difficult part is for Eisler to explain, first of all, why human society abandoned its pre-historical Eden for the nasty, brutish, short life offered by foreign marauders and, second of all, how contemporary society can reorganize along the lines of the partnership model.

In answering these questions about cultural transformation, Eisler gets to be slightly tough going. Not that she isn't supremely lucid at all times. It's just that the conceptual framework she uses to explain the massive systems shift from partnership to dominator is borrowed from recent theories about systems and the dynamics of change. In contrast to the linear, static models of old-fashioned science, which concentrate on the status quo, these new theories posit systems composed of self-organizing, interrelated, mutually reinforcing, mutually replicating components. Given the right set of circumstances, these systems can be upset to such a degree that their behavior becomes less and less predictable. Randomness increases until it reaches what scientists call "a critical bifurcation point" where the system has the capacity to transform itself into something completely different.

Eisler theorizes that the several millennia it took to shift from partnership society to dominator society was one such bifurcation point in human history. She also claims that we are, in the late twentieth century, on the verge of another such juncture. Humankind is faced with two drastic, diametrically opposed options: We can annihilate ourselves, or we can change our ideas. The reason why hopelessness is one of the major themes of the nuclear age is that, according to the logic of the dominator model, wars must inevitably occur. The next war will be our last, a fact that gets lost as the superpowers haggle over how many medium-range missiles to park in Europe.

Eisler proposes that we change our ideas instead. (One of the nice things about *The Chalice and the Blade* is that Eisler does not thump around like a prophet disseminating the Absolute Truth. She presents her ideas as something the reader might want to consider.) Many people have already changed their ideas—peace activists, ecologists, feminists, Gorbachev—but many more need to do so before large-scale shifts are possible.

Change *is* possible. At a given point in the past, it happened. Eisler shows how the dominators not only conquered the more peaceful communities physically, but also took the raw material of the partnership society—myths. technologies, belief systems —and transformed it to suit their radically different needs. At a definite period in the past, "knowledge became bad, birth became dirty, and death became a holy thing."

For instance, she takes the symbol of the snake. In early partnership societies it was the sign of feminine power and wisdom. Under dominator influence it became the reptile that precipitated man's fall, and it continues to be a symbol of malevolent female power, as the Medusa head and *The Witches of Eastwick* demonstrate. In this manner, *The Chalice and the Blade* offers drastic re-readings of Greek literature, Jesus, the medieval church, Marx, Freud ("a brilliant analyst of the dominator psyche, *not* the human psyche"), and Reagan's attachment to Iran (the linkage of two powerfully regressive dominator regimes).

Eisler believes that, for ideological reasons, the knowledge of our partnership past has been kept hidden or deliberately misinterpreted. In a recent interview with the *Weekly*, she said:

"We have been led to believe, in what is truly the biggest cover-up in the world, that we don't have this history—even though the clues are there. I mean, the Garden of Eden once existed. We have been led to believe that it's divinely ordained, or genetically ordained, that we live in a dominator system.... This knowledge, these models, I find to be very useful tools because I no longer find myself thinking there's no hope. We can only actualize our ideas if we think it's desirable and feasible—and that's the real purpose of the cover-up. Twentieth-century nihilism is a way of maintaining the dominator system."

In her talk at the International Synergy Institute in late May, Eisler stated that the three themes of *The Chalice and the Blade* are peace, partnership, and creativity. Of these three, her points on creativity are the most nebulous. Her theory is that true creativity, which she distinguishes from mere inventiveness, flourishes in partnership societies, while it is more or less suppressed in dominator societies. As exceptions, she cites the artists of the Renaissance and the Impressionists, creative in terms of their spontaneity, their joyfulness, their use of color, and their very immediate connection to nature.

The fact is, in the aesthetic realm, it's very difficult to "prove" Eisler's argument. Fortunately, Eisler intends to write three more volumes to flesh out and buttress the arguments made in *The Chalice and the Blade*.

In the meantime, read *The Chalice and the Blade*. It might make the future possible.

Organizations

The Center for Partnership Studies

Following publication of *The Chalice and the Blade*, response to the book's partnership model as a unifying framework for our lives was immediate and catalytic. Partnership discussion groups sprang up all over the country. Letters poured in from both men and women telling how the book's new information and concepts were changing their lives.

We founded the Center for Partnership Studies (CPS) in response to this wave of interest in the book's new perspective on our past and present, and the potential for a better future offered by the partnership model. CPS is committed to the realization of a partnership future, and with it, a more sustainable way of life. Since 1987, with the help of many committed volunteers, CPS has sought to accelerate the shift from domination to partnership with three main objectives.

- Information and Education

  Articles, books, tapes, and other materials for discussion and study listed in the CPS Resources Brochure and web page

  Partnership-based curriculum guidelines for primary, secondary, and university classes

  Pilot educational programs with universities and community education groups

- Research

  In-house research on effective strategies to restore balance to our lives and our planet

  Sponsorship of international research to further a global partnership future

  Development of new social inventions that give institutional value to partnership

- Action

  Cocreation with the Global Futures Foundation of a Clearinghouse on New Economic Inventions

Development of curricula and workshops with the International Partnership Network

Cosponsorship of national and international conferences on partnership

CPS is a 501(c)(3) nonprofit organization. A major source of funding for CPS is private donations, and these donations are tax deductible. If you want more information about CPS or any of its activities, to get on its mailing list, or to make a donation, write to:

The Center for Partnership Studies (P.O. Box 51936, Pacific Grove, California 93950) or visit our website at <www.partnershipway.org>

The International Partnership Network

Del Jones, Coordinator

The International Partnership Network (IPN) was started by women and men working together to advance the cultural transformation movement. We are dedicated to societal change: moving our society from a dominator model to a partnership model — from power over to power to and with, from ranking to linking, from violence to creative cooperation, from inequity to equity in gender, class, and age, and from disrespect to respect for the earth.

The International Partnership Network is an active membership organization for anyone whose life has been changed and inspired by the concepts and values in *The Chalice and the Blade*. As members, we are Partnership Educators and Partnership Practitioners. We are committed to changing our own behaviors, relationships, organizations, and our society as a whole, to reflect partnership, not domination.

We share our enthusiasm for partnership values with friends, co-workers, and other organizations. We organize study groups, plan conferences and workshops, linking with other organizations with similar goals and values. Together, we work in partnership, building a better tomorrow.

Since IPN has members spread all over the world, The Partnership Bulletin is our key means of communication, along with an email listfile and the internet home page (www.partnershipway.org). We also have a bi-annual training conference and are linked with Prescott College of Arizona in a Partnership Studies program.

Riane Eisler and David Loye are advisors to the International Partnership Network, a 501(c)(3) nonprofit organization.

For more information, please write to The International Partnership Network (P.O. Box 323, Tucson, Arizona 85702); email: delmeraz@aol.com; phone: (520)298-6542; fax: (520)298-0639

Acknowledgments

One of the pleasures of doing this book was that it came out of a true partnership process with many wonderful people who generously gave of their time and talent.

For providing vital experience and expertise in formulating the book's plan and working closely with us on it, we are especially grateful to Hannah Liebmann, Henry Holt, Isolina Ricci, Robin Van Doren, and Kali Furlong.

For their invaluable contributions to the section Additional Exercises and Topics for Discussion, we want to thank Karen-Elise Clay, Lethea F. Erz, Mici Gold, Linda Grover, Carol Haag, Sandra Heywood, Del Jones, Ron Kurtz, Jennifer Macleod, Arthur Melville, Carmen Montecinos, Harry Morel, Ruthmary Powers, Ann Moliver Ruben, Christine Sleeter, Vivian Swearingen, Marsha Utain, and Gail Van Buuren.

For the artwork, which so beautifully captures the spirit of both past and present and helps tell the story of who we were, are, and can be, we thank John Mason, Jeff Helwig, Jim Beeman, and John Thompson. We also want to thank Carmen Thompson-Wilson for her counsel and helpful sketches.

For additional support in all the many ways that make the big difference in partnership creativity, we want to express our appreciation to Elizabeth Anastos, Elinor Artman, Michael Boblett, Emily Caperton, Jean Darragh, Shelley Jackson Denham, Nancy Ferraro, Mara Keller, Jim Kenney, Christa Landon, Karuna Licht, Valera Lyles, June Martin, Janet Morrow, Vicki Noble, Mignonette Pellegrin, Linda Pinti, Lesley Phillips, Tracey Robinson-Harris, Caty Tannehill, Jane Van Velson, and Barbara White.

Our special thanks also to our agent Ellen Levine and Jan Johnson, the editor of the first edition of this book, and to Sherrin Bennett and Jeanne Gibbs for their early encouragement. We also want to especially thank Shirley Ranck for her important input as well as for her (and the Unitarian Universalists') permission to adapt portions of the Guidelines for Leaders from *Cakes for the Queen of Heaven*.

Last but certainly not least we want to thank all those who contributed to the revised second edition of this book: Charles Jakiela of the Holistic Education Press, Rob Koegel for his Foreword (and friendship over many years), and Heather Peet and Hannah Liebmann for their good ideas, personal support, and practical help.

Finally, we want to thank all those whose names are too numerous to list who have supported this endeavor both directly and through the Center for Partnership Studies.

Visit

www.sover.net/~holistic

on the Worldwide Web

for Additional Current

Partnership Way

Resources